T0285391

"High achievers live for the moments when we make the impossible possible. But for the moments that come before this—the late nights, poor habits, and sometimes heavy mindsets—Erin Stafford's *The Type A Trap* reminds us how to nurture ourselves outside of achievement to ensure we can move forward with the balance, clarity, and self-respect we need to continue changing the world."

CHRIS BARTON, founder of Shazam and serial entrepreneur

"Erin Stafford writes expertly on the delicate balance high achievers must master to honor both their dreams and their well-being. Her mindset shifts, paired with her witty personal stories, take readers on a journey to bring them back to themselves, one mindset shift at a time. Every Type A high achiever needs this book."

JOSH LINKNER, *New York Times* bestselling author, serial tech entrepreneur, and venture capital investor

"*The Type A Trap* is more than a book. It's a wise, hilarious best friend who knows how to set you straight and keep you smiling, both at work and at home."

LISI HARRISON, #1 *New York Times* bestselling author

"*The Type A Trap* is more than a personal development book—it is a powerful catalyst for self-discovery. Erin Stafford effortlessly blends candid personal stories with timely and relevant industry trends that illuminate a path toward our highest potential and happiness. If you've ever struggled to stay connected and present in your pursuit of excellence . . . you need this book."

SUNEEL GUPTA, bestselling author of *Backable* and *Everyday Dharma*

THE TYPE A TRAP

an imprint of Amplify Publishing Group

www.amplifypublishinggroup.com

For more information, please contact:
Amplify Publishing, an imprint of Amplify Publishing Group
620 Herndon Parkway, Suite 220
Herndon, VA 20170
info@amplifypublishing.com

Library of Congress Control Number: 2023909060

CPSIA Code: PRV01023A

ISBN-13: 978-1-63755-546-0

Printed in the United States

To my parents, who have given me unconditional love
and the confidence to believe I can do anything.

ERIN STAFFORD

THE
TYPE

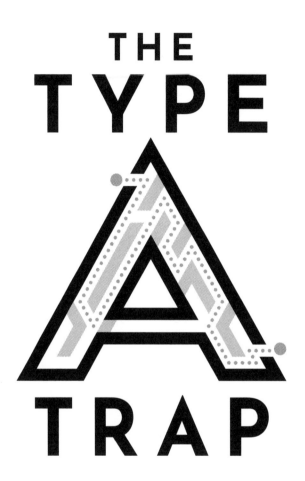

TRAP

Five Mindset Shifts to Beat Burnout and Transform Your Life

an imprint of Amplify Publishing Group

CONTENTS

AUTHOR'S NOTE

Hi, friend.

I'm so excited you're here!

If you're anything like me, you're probably feeling a little burned out, and you're wondering what to do about it. Maybe this is new territory for you, and you're in full panic mode. Or perhaps you know this feeling all too well and are looking for new techniques to combat it. Either way, this book is for you. It is chock-full of mindset shifts, tools, tactics, personal stories, and examples to help you not only prevent and overcome burnout but also sustain peak performance. I want you to get back to that feeling of absolutely kicking ass and thriving again. You know, that feeling you've had before but seem to have lost lately?

I've been exactly where you are and used each of these tools myself. I break them all down for you and know they work. You will be a different person after you read this book. All you have to do is actually do the work and take action.

But I know you. You're a motivated overachiever. I know you can do it.

You are just a few pages away from a whole new life. One that is happier, healthier, more balanced, and more fun.

You've got this my friend, and I can't wait to see the new you on the other side.

xoxo,
Erin

PART I

Burnout and the
Type A Personality

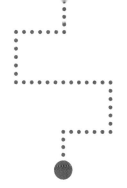

AN INTRODUCTION TO BURNOUT AND THE TYPE A PERSONALITY

From as early as I can remember, I've always been outgoing, opinionated, fiercely independent, hardworking, and someone who has never had a problem speaking her mind. It's just who I am. It's in my DNA. I was born this way and haven't changed. I can thank my mom for it, because as outspoken as I am, I'm a toned-down version of her. Let's just say, you always know exactly where you stand with her and what she's thinking. Her face and her mouth never lie. But I'd take that any day over walking around on eggshells, always unsure of what someone is thinking.

I was born with a ridiculous sense of self-confidence that has allowed me to do the most audacious things—not because I wasn't scared or didn't have imposter syndrome, but because I knew I wanted to accomplish that thing and would do whatever I needed to do to make it happen. Sure, I got scared just like everyone else, but I did it anyway. Like the time I became a celebrity stylist by answering an ad on Craigslist. Or the time I got a job in a newsroom by teaching myself how to edit video by watching YouTube and BSing my way through the interview.

I've had some pretty awesome jobs over the years, and all of them have happened because I've set my sights on something, worked my ass off, got creative in my approach, networked, schmoozed, and figured out a way to make it happen.

It's been amazing and so much fun to experience. It's given me the highest of the highs, and, until the pandemic, this quality made me think that I was invincible. I could do anything. I could accomplish *anything*. All I had to do was put in some hard work, and, if I did it long enough, I would eventually achieve my goal. After all, that's what I'd done my whole life.

But everything changed a year into the pandemic. A laundry list of things happened that dumped me into a dark hole—one I'd never been in before and didn't know how to get out of. All of my usual tactics of just working harder didn't work. In fact, they made me feel even worse. The most devastating thing that happened during this time was my fertility journey. "Infertility journey" is more like it, but *infertility* is a word I don't like to use often, because it feels so final and hopeless. Maybe I'm delusional, but I like to still have hope.

I always thought since I was healthy, not overweight, ate well, and took care of myself that when my husband and I were ready to have kids, we'd be able to. Looking back now, I can hardly type that without laughing. How naive I was!

Since I was in my late thirties and my husband was in his early forties, we knew we were already pushing our luck age-wise—especially me. But forge ahead we did. After trying naturally for a few months to no avail, we decided to take the most direct route and do in vitro fertilization (IVF).

So off we waltzed to the fertility clinic with our checkbooks out and hope in our hearts. One round, two rounds, three rounds of IVF later, and we still couldn't seem to buy a baby. All our tests came back healthy, and there was no identifiable reason why it wasn't working. But in fact, there was. I was burned out beyond measure—my body was in survival mode, and there was no way it was physically able to do anything other than exist.

What I didn't realize at the time was the deep connection and complex relationship that exists between stress, exhaustion, and our physical health. I was doing everything right (so I thought), but my body was failing me.

I was tired. Like tired at the *soul* level. Nothing made me happy. I felt like I was living life in a total fog. I'm usually such a high energy, happy person, and, all of a sudden, I was just drifting through life at the lowest possible energy level. Nothing excited me. Nothing fired me up. It was as if my car was stuck in neutral, unable to move forward or backward. Just stuck in blasé land. Trapped.

I realized that all of the things that had made me successful throughout my life—the hustle, grind, long hours, fixation on achievement—were actually the things that were causing me to, dare I say, *burn out*. It was a trap I'd never been in before and one I didn't even know existed. It was the beginning of discovering the Type A Trap.

I knew I needed to make some changes in my life. Changes I'd never made before. I was in a trap and didn't know how to get out. But like any good overachiever, I was determined to find a way out.

Exhausted, frazzled, stressed—these were all terms I'd heard before and could relate to. But *burnout*? Hard pass. That had nothing to do with me.

But after enough research and talking to others, I realized I was indeed burned out. My first thought was, *Well, this is embarrassing! I'm too hardworking and good at what I do to burn out. I eat well and exercise and get plenty of sleep; how could I be burned out?*

Maybe you've been there too. Maybe you've gone through life doing all the "right" things. Gotten good grades, gone to college, excelled in your career, been a loving partner and super parent, exercised regularly, ate well, bought the house, took the vacations, all the things. Yet slowly things start to disintegrate. Slowly bits and pieces of your life are breaking down like sand pouring through your fingers; no matter how hard you try to hold on, you just can't. And finally, you wake up one day feeling like a completely different person. Someone you don't recognize.

According to the American Institute of Stress, 33 percent of people report feeling stress at extreme levels. Seventy-seven percent of people experience stress to the point of it affecting their physical health, and 73 percent experience stress that impacts their mental health in significant ways.[1]

It can start small and seemingly insignificant, like unnecessary road rage. I'm from Southern California and have spent so much of my life in traffic, so I know about unnecessary road rage all too well. If you do not accelerate the *microsecond* that the light turns green, I'm the girl giving you a courtesy honk to get you moving along. It's terrible, but it's true. If you are dawdling and not driving fast enough, I'm saying things under my breath to you in the car and trying to pass you, even if I'm not in a hurry and have nowhere I need to be. The struggle to keep this in check is real.

Early signs of burnout could be snapping at people, drinking more than usual, zoning out during conference calls, having trouble concentrating, or, my personal favorite, letting other people respond to group emails. How many times have you gotten an email with seven people on it, and you think to yourself, *I don't feel like dealing with this. I'll let the others respond. If they call me out specifically, I'll respond, otherwise, I'll just let it go.* Another favorite is the mouse jiggle. You know, when you're sitting at your desk, and you're not really doing anything, but every now and then you jiggle your mouse just to make sure you stay "active" on Microsoft Teams or whatever messaging system your company uses. I've done this more times than I can count.

Burnout can quickly progress to having anxiety, missing deadlines, failing project launches, feeling apathetic, and sabotaging relationships. I know my burnout is getting worse when all of a sudden, every single thing my husband does (or doesn't do) annoys the hell out of me. From the way he's breathing or chewing his food to the way he shakes his hands after he washes them and spritzes water everywhere to the way he folds the towels the "wrong" way. It doesn't matter what it is, it annoys me when I'm in the throes of burnout, when most of the time it doesn't. Actually, I lie. The water spritzing always bothers me.

And if you don't address burnout, it can lead to depression, panic disorder, losing your job, or serious illnesses like high blood pressure, heart attacks, and cancer. Sadly, I know of a number of highly successful Type A people who lead companies or have senior roles in them who have been diagnosed with cancer at a young age when they are otherwise healthy. While I don't know the details of their cases, it's hard not to think that the stress of their jobs and their constant go-go-go attitude contributed to their cancer diagnoses.

As you can see, burnout can affect every area of your life! Unfortunately, we can't just work out like maniacs and eat well for one day or week and instantly be in killer shape. It doesn't work that way. It can take years to lose weight and get healthy. We must consistently and regularly eat well and exercise in order to stay healthy and in shape. Think of preventing and overcoming burnout in the same way. It isn't a one-and-done thing. Our efforts, for anything in life, compound. We've made many decisions and taken on habits over months and years that lead us to how we feel and operate today.

But it doesn't have to be this way. We've been so bombarded by a hustle-and-grind culture that it's hard to even think about what it feels like to be rested, peaceful, and happy. And it gets even harder to remember that it's possible and even our birthright to not be in a constant state of high stress. You don't have to run yourself into the ground; risk losing your job; and put your health, your financial stability, your family, and relationships in jeopardy in order to reach the highest levels of success. The old path to success is in the past, and there's a new, nontraditional way of excelling and reaching peak performance without burning out. And I'm going to share that with you in these pages.

A life completely free of stress doesn't exist (as much as we'd like it to). We'd be naive to think that would ever happen. It's learning how to spot burnout, treat it, and prevent it that is key. I know it may be hard to imagine right now, but it's possible to fall asleep and stay asleep every night without taking a cocktail of melatonin and CBD. To wake up rested. To have energy throughout the day without ten cups of coffee. It's possible to be an incredible leader without being the first one in and last one out and saying yes to every single new project or initiative that comes your way. It's possible to be a present parent and partner without constantly feeling like you're barely alive or failing. It's possible to show up for your family and friends while still making time for yourself. And it's possible to spot the early warning signs that you're getting off track and starting to burn out and course-correct before it's too late.

Is it easy? No. Is it possible? Yes.

I hate to break it to you, but you're not going to read this book and instantly be cured. If it were that easy, we wouldn't have millions of burned-out people. Burnout is something that requires constant attention and consistent action. And this book will give you the tools and mindset shifts to use throughout your days and weeks to set you on a path to keep burnout at bay both in the short and long term. Think of this book as your burnout personal trainer to keep you in shape mentally.

There is a way to come back to yourself. A way to get back to feeling good about yourself and your accomplishments. To find some balance between the success and the exhaustion. To continue to stay at the level of high-performance you're used to, without the burnout. Because if we're too tired or sick to enjoy the success we've worked so hard for, then what's the point?

I wrote the book I wish I had read years ago. A book that was written for leaders, Type A personalities, perfectionists, over-achievers, peak performers, and success-obsessed individuals. For the frazzled folks trying to do it all, who put everyone first before themselves. I hope this book not only helps you feel seen and understood, but that it gives you practical tools you can put to use in your own life as well as share with your teams so that you can all live happier, healthier lives.

This book is organized into three sections. After setting the stage with an overview of burnout and the Type A personality, I'll share a comprehensive burnout quiz to assess your level of burnout today. It's essential to know where you are now so that you can plan your escape out of the Type A Trap accordingly.

Next, I break down five simple, yet incredibly effective, mindset shifts that take you from feeling lost and burned out in the Type A Trap to kicking ass and thriving again on the other side. Now, as we know, what is simple is not always easy. But I break each shift down into practical steps and give you countless examples and suggestions on how to implement each shift in your life. Please don't feel like you have to do everything I suggest. I simply include a lot of options because we're all so different. What appeals to one person may not appeal to another, and I want to make sure everyone who reads this book feels like they get something out of it and knows how to implement the shifts in their real life.

Mindset Shift #1 Is to Decode Your Flow. Type As have a tendency to try to master everything no matter what, even if all that mastery does little to move them forward. This shift will teach you how to intentionally select how you spend your time, so you know your most precious resource is being spent on what truly matters and fills your cup.

Mindset Shift #2 Is to Release the Reins. A textbook sign of the Type A Trap is a fierce need for control and relentless micromanaging. This shift empowers you to release this need to control everything in your life, helping you trust others in your community to work alongside you.

Mindset Shift #3 Is to Pivot Like a Pro. Type As are planners. And we're really good at it. We get stuff done. However, sometimes our devotion to our plans can backfire. Our need to stay the course no matter what is not always a strength. This shift will teach you how to pivot and move with agility when you feel that something is no longer serving you.

Mindset Shift #4 Is to Slow Down to Speed Up. Taking action, getting things done, and maximizing time are qualities that bring Type As so much of their success. But this incessant need for movement and progress comes at a cost—usually to our health, relationships, and sometimes sanity. This shift will coach you on how to stop feeling like you need to max out every minute of your time to get results and start embracing planning for the long term, which includes respecting self-care and rest so you can perform at your best when it matters.

Mindset Shift #5 Is to Take a Victory Lap. Instead of the constant *go, go, go, win, what's next* mentality that leads us to burnout, we need to celebrate our progress, savor the wins, and show gratitude. This shift will teach you how to pause and acknowledge your progress and accomplishments in a way you haven't allowed yourself to do before.

While I was struggling in the throes of burnout, I knew there were people out there who had gone through what I was experiencing and had unique perspectives and lessons to share to help me and others. To support my own experience, I interviewed dozens and dozens of high achievers from all different walks of life. People like the Guinness World Records holder for world's fittest man, leading doctors and lawyers, celebrity coaches, retired US Navy SEAL captains, and three-time Olympians. I also surveyed thousands of people from across the United States to find out how they stay at peak performance without burning out. I've taken all that data and distilled it into many of the concepts I share in these pages. Throughout this book, I've included Trap Talk sections, which share stories from many of the high achievers I interviewed who have all confronted their own versions of burnout in their personal lives and careers.

I also sought out the opinions of exceptional mental health experts in the field of stress and burnout. I have deep personal experience and several years of research and speaking under my belt on this topic, but I am not a mental health expert or physician. Throughout the book, you'll see Psyched! sections sharing professional insights from two incredible psychologists: Dr. Madelyn Blair and Dr. Marsha Chinichian, as well as Dr. Darria Long, an emergency room physician who helped lead the largest study on burnout in women in the country in conjunction with Dr. Christopher Cunningham and Dr. Kristen Black, two industrial organizational psychologists from the University of Tennessee at Chattanooga. Their thoughts on the topics shared in this book are invaluable to anyone's journey toward healing burnout, anxiety, and panic. I encourage you to use their perspectives as well as the rest of this book as a springboard to investigating other mental health resources—such as seeking out a therapist or counselor or even simply learning more about psychology.

The book concludes with a couple chapters on how to sustain peak performance and keep burnout at bay when, without fail, the Type A Trap continues to test us.

This book will help you feel seen and understood. It will show you that you're not alone, and there's nothing wrong with you. What you're going through is very normal and something that millions of others deal with as well. It will leave you with countless corporate and personal examples of the mindset shifts in action and will arm you with a toolkit of tactics to use to keep yourself out of the Type A Trap and thriving in both business and life. Most importantly, it will give you hope. Hope that there IS a way out. That it is possible to be successful and happy and not burned out. They are not mutually exclusive. There is indeed a way out of the trap, and you can and will get through it. So, let's get started!

The Type A Personality Explained

Type A personalities have a special, complex, and intimate relationship with burnout. I'm going to assume that since you picked up this book, the title caught your eye, and you might already relate to or consider yourself to be Type A. It's important to remember that most things in life are on a scale. Some people may feel they exhibit the Type A personality in every area of their lives, while others may feel they align with it only in certain areas or seasons of their lives.

While there is no official definition, in general, Type A personalities are extroverted, extremely internally motivated, and competitive overachievers. They tend to be entrepreneurs and CEOs, executive leaders, professional athletes and Olympians, trial lawyers, and performers, among other things. Type As inspire others and are highly productive, goal achievers, and critical thinkers. They're often the life of the party and have a genuine joy for life and infectious energy. They're the ones who organize all the family and friend get-togethers, they're the default team leaders for any activity no matter how big or small, and the ones who many look to and think, *How do they do it all?*

Type A behavior can also show up as perfectionist tendencies—like the mom who obsesses over what goes into her kid's lunch box or the clean freak who has to have everything in the house just so. Type As can also be micromanagers or control freaks who are unable to let go and trust others to get the job done. They can sometimes be unsympathetic and intolerant of excuses or people who slow them and their goals down. I'm sure we all know people like this.

Below is a list of common Type A behaviors and characteristics. While this list is by no means exhaustive, it should be enough to give you an idea of the Type A personality and what drives them.

Type A Characteristics	
Self-motivated	Natural leader
Outgoing	Fast-paced
Extroverted	Passionate
Competitive	Entrepreneurial
Extremely ambitious	Demands flexibility and autonomy
Defines success by accomplishments	Embraces change well
Tends to multitask	High level of self-control
Hates wasting time	Decisive and direct
Impatient	Not afraid to take risks
Workaholic	Highly independent
Highly focused on goals	Controlling

According to WebMD, Type A "refers to a pattern of behavior and personality associated with high achievement, competitiveness, and impatience."[2] But the term actually originated in a study by two cardiologists named Friedman and Rosenman, who discovered the behavior type by accident in 1976.[3]

The cardiologists needed their waiting room chairs reupholstered much sooner than expected. When they called in an expert to do the job, the upholsterer said he had never seen chairs wear in this type of pattern before. Unlike most people who wait patiently in the seats at the doctor's office, it looked like the people waiting in the cardiologists' office weren't actually sitting in the chairs for very long. Instead, they would perch themselves on the edge of the seat and get up and down frequently, wearing out the very edge of the seat and the armrests instead of the middle.

The cardiologists ignored this remark at first, but five years later, they began formal research on the personality types of their patients and found that those they classified as "Type A" were more than twice as likely to have heart disease and high blood pressure than those who were type B, who happened to be more relaxed, patient, and easy going.[4] Unfortunately, the study only included men, so their results lack well-rounded insights that indicate patterns in all humans. Although their research has since been debunked because it failed to include women, the term "Type A" has stuck and is still in regular use today. Identifying with the Type A personality isn't an automatic fast pass to stress, but Type A personalities are at a greater risk of suffering from burnout.

The Burnout Epidemic

The term *burnout* was first used in the 1970s by an American psychologist named Herbert Freudenberger who used it to describe the consequences of severe stress for people in what he calls "helping professions," such as doctors and nurses.[5] But unlike traditional diseases or ailments, there is no concrete definition for burnout. It's classified as an occupational hazard by the World Health Organization, and defined by them as:

> ...[A] syndrome conceptualized as resulting from chronic workplace stress that has not been successfully managed. It is characterized by three dimensions:
>
> - feelings of energy depletion or exhaustion;
> - increased mental distance from one's job, or feelings of negativism or cynicism related to one's job; and
> - reduced professional efficacy.[6]

Depending on what article you read or source you consult, you'll likely get a different definition. But they are all generally the same. Burnout is a term used for anyone who is under extreme stress and shows exhaustion, alienation/detachment from work, and reduced performance.[7]

But while it started as a term for a particular industry, it can affect anyone from stay-at-home parents and shift workers to executives and athletes. Since experts don't agree on exactly what burnout is, it makes it difficult to diagnose and quantify how many people have it.[8]

Take a look at any news station or media outlet, and you'll see countless stories on burnout and the Great Resignation. They usually go hand in hand. The US Bureau of Labor Statistics (BLS) reports that at the peak, 4.5 million people quit their jobs in November 2021.[9] And as I write this in 2022, more than 4 million Americans are quitting their jobs every month.[10] These are the highest numbers ever seen since the BLS started recording this data more than twenty years ago!

According to Indeed, employee burnout is on the rise. Fifty-two percent of all workers feel burned out, and 67 percent say their burnout increased during the pandemic.[11] It's no surprise. We took an already exhausted workforce, gave them more work and longer hours, isolated them, took away their support system, and added homeschooling and taking care of aging parents to their plate. Add on to that the uncertainty of a global pandemic, and it's no wonder everyone is burned out and quitting!

Not only are people quitting their jobs and changing careers at levels never seen before, but according to Gallup, 51 percent are not engaged in their work.[12] These are the quiet quitters—people who are burned out but who can't leave their jobs for whatever reason. They're disengaged, emotionally removed from the work, no longer invested in it, and are doing the absolute bare minimum to get by to remain employed but still have some semblance of their lives back.

We're constantly stuck in the Type A Trap. As a society, we're conditioned to believe that achievement, often in the form of salary and job title, is everything. That's the pervasive message we're told again and again. Success equals money and power. And as motivated people who want to succeed, we work and work. But what helps us achieve at the highest levels early on in our career can be the very thing that contributes to our downfall later.

The same goes for other areas of our lives. We want to be the perfect parent, so we throw the Pinterest-worthy birthday parties, volunteer at school, and make healthy lunches that include a personal note every day. We plan the family Halloween costumes and picture-perfect holiday cards and do all the things. But it runs us into the ground, and ultimately all our kids remember is whether we built a fort or played in the pool with them.

Wherever you are in your life—student, early in your career, single, married, a parent or a caretaker—Type As tend to want to do everything well. So well that it ends up being what sends us into the Type A Trap and burnout. We work so much without a break and wear our work ethic like a badge of honor, until we run ourselves into the ground and burn out. Sometimes we decide to make a surface-level change, like jumping to a new job or cutting out a few tasks here and there. But the issue is our mindset is still the same, and we end up right back where we were.

If we find a new job or shift one aspect of our busy schedules without changing any of our behaviors or mindsets, we're simply running away. We're just changing locations and bringing all our old problems along with us like that extra ten pounds we just can't seem to shake. We'll just burn out again at our next gig.

How many times have you tried one diet, but you didn't stick to it and went right back to your old ways? Or tried a new exercise regime, but you petered out after a couple of days and went back to your previous sedentary life? Or you find yourself constantly dating the same type of person, even though you know the relationship is toxic and keeping you stuck? Sure, they may look different and have a different name, but your relationship has all the same issues as the last one. If we don't change anything about our behavior, mindset, or beliefs about ourselves and our lives, we'll stay stuck in this constant state of stagnation and burnout. Nothing will change unless we change it.

Aren't you tired of being tired? Aren't you ready to have more free time on your hands? Free time where you're actually relaxing and not just trying to relax while feeling guilty for relaxing. Aren't you ready to be a more present parent? To actually have the time, and, more importantly, the energy to be there for your kids, not just when they need you, but to make memories in the day-to-day moments, which tend to be the most special and memorable anyway? Aren't you ready to be a more loving partner? To not snap at your partner at the drop of a hat, to be able to receive love and give it freely and easily? To go out of your way to make them happy simply because you can, not because you've been working ridiculous hours and now feel obligated to?

You deserve this reality and more.

It's so easy to bury the warning signs and tell ourselves and everyone else that we're the dreaded F word—*fine*. But the truth is, ignoring burnout never lasts. Eventually it will catch up to you, usually at the most inopportune times. It could take the form of gallstones, a panic attack, a miscarriage, or any number of other things—none of which are fun.

If we don't take the time to proactively address and attend to our physical and mental health, we're on the fast train to burnout with a one-way ticket. Checking in with yourself and honestly questioning where your stress levels are is invaluable in staying healthy and aligned in your life.

In order to help you evaluate your level of burnout, take the time to go through the burnout assessment in the next section. Having this information before we dive into the mindset shifts will empower you to embrace these ideas and make the necessary changes in your life. Make this the day you take back control of your time, your energy, and your health. What are you waiting for?

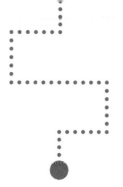

BURNOUT ASSESSMENT

Burnout shows up in an alarming number of ways. It's a cunning thief that robs the world of its best and its brightest by feeding on our energy, enthusiasm, and passion, then transforming these positive qualities into exhaustion, frustration, and disillusionment.[1]

But most people suffering with this think they're not burned out. You may be one of the people who think burnout only happens to *those* people, but the truth is burnout is incredibly deceiving, often lurking just underneath the surface, waiting to attack when you least expect it. And it takes a lot of time, effort, tears, and money to pull yourself out.

As I mentioned earlier, there is no official way to diagnose burnout. Instead, it is helpful to take a holistic look at all the areas of your life to get a pulse-check on your stress level. In this assessment, I've outlined six areas of life. Obviously there are others, but the answers to these questions should be able to give you a very good idea as to your current level of burnout.

I know you might want to just skip this part and move on to the next chapter, but don't! It's important to understand where you are now, so you can address it and be open to the tools outlined in this book so you can move past burnout to thriving on the other side.

Go get a pen right now and take a minute to review the list of symptoms below. Circle all the ones that you're currently experiencing, then count your total. Consult the score explanations at the end of this section.

Health	
Trouble sleeping	Forgetting why you walked into a room
Racing thoughts	Anxiety
Constant exhaustion	Apathy
Change in diet	Crying regularly
Using food/alcohol/drugs to cope	High blood pressure
No energy	Heart disease/attack
Skin issues like rosacea, eczema, or dermatitis that won't go away	Cancer
Irritability	Infertility
Depression	No motivation to exercise
Bloating	Binge eating
Constipation/diarrhea	Regular headaches
Auto-immune issues	Muscle tension
Low energy level	Eating poorly
Brain fog	Drinking too much
Trouble focusing	Nerve pain

Work	
Zoning out	Over-delegating to team
Missing deadlines	Letting other people respond to group emails
Getting written up	Joining calls late
Phoning it in	Failing projects
Not contributing during meetings or calls	Losing your job
Quiet quitting/doing the bare minimum	Feeling like all you do is work, yet you don't accomplish enough
Being online, but not present	Detaching from work
Not responding to emails	Cynical about work and colleagues
Abdicating responsibilities	Lacking creativity

Faith/Spirituality	
Feeling hopeless	Don't find joy in your spiritual practice anymore
Feeling like there is no purpose to life	Feeling like your spiritual guide has abandoned you
Isolating yourself from your spiritual community	Feeling like your spiritual guide is far away from you
No time for prayer/ meditation/spiritual practice	Experiencing spiritual doubt
Thinking your higher power doesn't love you/has forgotten you/isn't hearing your prayers	Avoiding your spiritual community

Family and Friends

Sabotaging relationships	Neediness
Isolating yourself	Resentful of doing things for your partner
Picking fights	Everything your partner does annoys you
Hypersensitivity	Every conversation turns into a fight
Not making time to see loved ones	Missing special events
Regular disagreements	Not being present with your kids
Lack of sex drive	Snapping regularly
Impassionate sex	Not confiding in your family/friends, thinking they don't understand
Aversion to physical affection	You take care of everyone, but they don't take care of you

Finances

Spending money frivolously	Making risky investments beyond your means
Overspending on coffees and meals out	Projecting a lifestyle you can't sustain
Ignoring budgets	Keeping up with the Joneses
Paying bills late	Getting loans for things you can't afford
Gambling	Racking up credit card debt

Fun	
Nothing feels fun anymore	Not taking time off for vacations/down time
Feeling like you have no time for fun	Unable to disconnect
Thinking everyone else is having fun except you	Feeling guilty for having fun/taking time off
Even when you make time for fun, you don't enjoy it	Always feeling like you have to accomplish something
Resentful of those having fun	Regularly checking your emails while outside of work hours
Envious of other people's lifestyles	Spending too much time on social media
Unable to relax	Abandoning hobbies

Results

0 to 33 – The Shallow End

Count your blessings, my friend, you're in far better shape than most. You may feel great in some areas and a little iffy in others, but overall, you're doing well and managing your stress. But it's a slippery slope and only takes one hard thing to bump you up to the next level, so I commend you for reading this book and learning new tools to prevent burnout before it becomes a bigger problem in your life. Of the six life areas detailed above, which one has the highest score? That is where to focus first. Try to incorporate a minimum of one to two of the mindset shifts into your life to avoid burning out.

34 to 67 – The Wake-Up Call

Think of this as your wake-up call at some ridiculously early hour of the morning. You're in trouble, and it's time to make some serious changes in your life. Stress is starting to consume your life, and you're likely seeing physical manifestations of it. Your work and your relationships are suffering. It is painful and not a fun place to live. You know this isn't how you want to feel but aren't sure what to do or where to start. Aim to incorporate at least three to four of the mindset shifts into your life to prevent you from ending up in the danger zone.

68 to 100 – The Danger Zone

This is the danger zone, and, sadly, a young Tom Cruise isn't coming to rescue you by putting you on the back of his motorcycle and driving off into the San Diego sunset. It will more likely be an ambulance ride strapped to a gurney with the blare of sirens taking you to the hospital. All six of the areas detailed in this assessment are hurting *badly*. Your body and mind are in agony. It's excruciating and no way to live your life. But there is a way out, and it's possible to break free from this burnout prison. Aim to incorporate all of the five mindset shifts into your life and as many of the tactics detailed in this book as possible. You're in hot water, and you need immediate change.

PART II

The Mindset Shifts

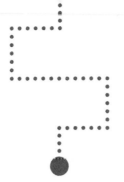

DECODE
YOUR FLOW

Instead of mastering everything no matter what, shift to deliberately selecting tasks that are the best use of your time.

A s motivated overachievers and peak performers, we believe we can do anything. And we can! We have a ridiculous sense of self-confidence and know that we can literally do, learn, and achieve whatever we put our minds to because we're willing to do the work necessary to be successful.

When I was thirty-six, I got an incredible job as the head of marketing for a large healthcare staffing company. I reported directly to the CEO and was in charge of every aspect of marketing, advertising, communications, public relations, creative, production, digital, etc., etc., etc. It was *a lot* and definitely overwhelming at times. When I started, there were only three people on the team. Six years later, I had grown the team to more than sixty-five people. Over that time, my work went from the basics of getting our company on the map, creating brand standards, improving our creative, and stopping the sales team from doing DIY marketing to managing multimillion-dollar budgets, launching new brands, and scouring data to see where we could continue to make improvements. The growth was insane, not just in my department, but in the whole company. We were a hyper-growth company that grew nine times in two years.

As the budgets got bigger and the stakes higher, I had to dig deeper into our digital strategy—after all, that's where the vast majority of our leads came from, so it was kinda important. But there was one problem; I'm a creative, not an analytical person. I was far more interested in creating the ads that would run on digital platforms—the copy, photos, fonts, layouts, and anima-tion—than interpreting or honestly even looking at how they actu-ally performed. Yet every week, my boss would hammer me on metrics that I felt unable to interpret. So, I did what any other Type A would do and tried to study my way into expertise. I went to digital conferences to learn the latest techniques, took online courses, read industry blogs regularly, had my team send me intri-cate reports, nearly went blind devouring Excel spreadsheets, and more. I tried to double down on all things digital to prove to my boss and myself that I was not only capable of overseeing digital but that I excelled at it. This is just how Type As operate. If we're going to do something, we're not going to half-ass it. We're going to go all in and do it well.

But this overextension and insistence on mastering everything no matter what keeps us in the Type A Trap—and it eventually leads to our downfall. It leads to exhaustion, struggling at work, and neglecting our relationships and our health. As a Type A personality, you're likely already scoping out if there is a better way, and there is . . . but it may feel counter-intuitive at first.

To prevent this fierce burnout, we need to shift our thinking from mastering everything, no matter what, to strict and methodical selection of what we spend our time on. I call this **decoding your flow.**

I tried for years to force something that ultimately wasn't my strength or interest. Every week, my team would send me reports that I'm sure were great and helpful, but as soon as I looked at them my eyes glazed over, and I wasn't totally sure what I was looking at. I knew I needed to do a better job, but I also ultimately realized that my time and energy were better spent elsewhere. I eventually decoded my flow and hired a digital director who lived and breathed digital. He was able to dramatically improve our digital performance almost immediately, when, despite my best efforts, I was barely moving the needle. And most importantly, he loved it, and I didn't, so I now had more time to devote to the things I enjoyed and was actually good at.

Talking Shift

Just as we've decoded our morning routine—ensuring our coffee has just the right amount of creamer, the temperature in the shower is exactly how we like it, and we get in the correct lane at precisely the right spot on the freeway to avoid congestion (being from Southern California, this is particularly important for my morning routine)—we need to think of decoding our flow the same way. We must ensure we are being thoughtful and methodical about how we spend our time. With our work ethic and insatiable drive to succeed, if we don't, our burnout will run us off our perfectly charted path. Decoding our flow helps us set our priorities so we spend time on the things that actually matter and bring us joy instead of doing things just because we don't want to look like a quitter, we don't want to let someone down, we feel obligated, someone expects us to, or we're living someone else's dream.

How many times have you found yourself doing something you really aren't interested in solely because someone else wants or expects you to? I didn't get married until I was forty-one, so let's just say I dated a LOT of guys before I found Mr. Right.

I can't tell you how many times in a budding relationship I'd find myself exaggerating my interest in something just to try to make whatever fledgling relationship I was in work. Watching football when I'd rather watch paint dry, drinking beer in a craft brewery when I'm definitely a wine girl, playing disc golf or tolerating terrible jokes from someone I just don't think is funny and missing out on quality time with my girlfriends or family in the hopes that maybe, just maybe, if I tried a little harder this guy would be *the one*.

I'd muster up all my energy to be excited about camping and sleeping in some mosquito-infested swamp when deep down, all I wanted was a bougie boutique hotel with a view and poolside cocktails. Without even realizing it, I was spending way too much energy pursuing something I didn't even want or like—taking trips to REI for beige, shapeless camping clothing that converts from pants to shorts with a quick zip; spending money on expensive hiking boots, and saying, "It's okay," when the lake we thought we could swim in is actually a reservoir that you're not allowed to touch so now there's nothing to do at the camp site. These moments happened so often in my dating life I had to ask myself if my future really did have a partner in it, if I had to keep compromising myself, or if I really had just not found Mr. Right yet. And this is just one example. I've done similar things in friendships and jobs that just weren't the right fit.

We have to continually ask ourselves if what we're doing and how we're spending our time is truly aligned with our goals, priorities, passions, and interests both at home and at work. Thankfully, there are methods to help us discover if we're as aligned as we think we are. Marie Kondo was onto something with her whole "Does it spark joy?" concept. If it doesn't, take that as a sign that it's time to decode your flow.

Inefficiencies Are Clues

On the job, inefficiencies are like small warning lights telling us there are opportunities to look closely and decode our flow to be more balanced and productive. If we're lucky, we notice these warning lights before they become huge issues. Hootsuite, the popular social media management software company, realized they needed to decode their flow when an employee wanted to send a customer a logoed cotton T-shirt. Nothing fancy, just a regular shirt with a Hootsuite logo on it. But by the time they went through all the approvals and accounted for everyone's time, the price of the shirt was more than $200!

Why? Because managers had to approve all company swag requests. Now this may have worked fine during Hootsuite's early days, but as the company grew to more than 1,000 employees, the process became cumbersome and completely unreasonable. This was the warning light.

They knew they needed a better way, so they created a "Czar of Bad Systems"—a new role with responsibility for observing processes and workflows, identifying which ones were inefficient or wasteful, and then either fixing or removing them.[1] Doesn't that sound good? I think every company I've ever worked for could use this role. My personal life could use a Czar of Bad Systems too! Lord knows there are plenty of outdated and inefficient processes there. For example, can someone please help me figure out a way to remember to bring the bags into the grocery store with me instead of constantly leaving them at home? I'm forever buying new bags every time I go to the store (because I live in California, and they are no longer free). But then I end up with a mountain of them under the kitchen sink collecting dust and getting in the way, only to buy more the next time because I've forgotten them. There must be a better way!

Hootsuite's Czar of Bad Systems updated the swag approval process, saving hundreds of employee hours a year just in ordering swag. The Czar of Bad Systems went on to decode the flow in many other areas of the organization to ensure employee time was spent where it was most profitable and productive.

Google and Facebook also regularly decode their flow (or decode their code, if you will). It's easy for us mere mortals to think of these enormous and iconic brands as doing nothing but succeeding in business. Sure, they've had, and continue to have, their share of legal and privacy issues, but if you look at their bottom line, they're both Silicon Valley powerhouses and the envy of many a failed tech start-up. But they're not insulated from the need to decode their flows. Both companies regularly launch products to great fanfare and media attention, only to quietly shutter them months or years later, never to be spoken about again. Hell, Elon Musk is currently decoding Twitter's flow as I write this book, although one could argue it's more of an unraveling than a decoding.

Google is notorious for axing poorly performing products. To memorialize all of Google's failed products (in exhaustive detail) and to make us all feel better about our failed businesses or projects, a front-end developer named Cody Ogden created Killed by Google—a site that lists all of Google's failed products. It's incredible to see just how many products Google creates—often releasing more in one year than many companies do in a decade. "Entrepreneurs find inspiration and renewed vigor in seeing a successful company like Google take a seemingly cutthroat approach to product development," says Ogden.[2] And it's true. There are just under three hundred failed products listed on the site—proof that there's something to the whole notion of throwing everything against the wall and seeing what sticks. Thankfully for Google, they've done a pretty good job at finding things that stick, but only after testing and trashing countless products. It's clear that they are consistently evaluating what product options are performing and adding value to customers and the business and cutting out anything that doesn't fit.

Facebook follows a similar approach. They constantly release new products, often as a direct result of a competitor encroaching on their audience.[3] But CEO Mark Zuckerberg is ruthless in killing off underperformers. Remember Facebook email, deals, credits, or gifts? Neither do I. They came and went faster than a bad date. And trust me, those guys split quick!

So, if Google and Facebook regularly toss out products that aren't successful, then yeah, that failed attempt to sell Rodan + Fields, LuLaRoe, or any other multilevel marketing (MLM) scheme you tried is nothing you can't recover from. The key here is to decode your flow and do it sooner rather than later. Fail fast and reevaluate. There's no point holding onto something that isn't working simply because you're too embarrassed to say it didn't work.

Spanx founder and CEO—and one of my favorite bad-ass entrepreneur inspirations—Sara Blakely, often talks about how her father would ask her and her siblings every day at the dinner table what they failed at that day. He would get upset if they hadn't failed at anything because that meant they weren't trying something new. And if they weren't trying something new, then they weren't growing. Just like Google and Facebook understand the importance of trying new things and failing fast to create a successful business, Mr. Blakely understood the value of failing in your personal life to decode your flow and how essential it is to ensuring you're working efficiently toward goals that align with your passion and dreams.

You Don't Have to Do It All

Trying to be everything and do everything never results in our best work or our best mental health, for that matter. We know that. We've heard it a million times. Yet, we still overextend and overbook (and often overdrink or overeat) to try to get it all done. By decoding our flow, we create intentionality and focus to direct our attention and energy on what lights us up and fuels our passions instead of what depletes us.

One concept that resonates on a deep level, but that I still struggle with, is focusing on efficiency over productivity. Like many high achievers, I'm productive AF. You want something done? I'll work my ass off to make it happen. But my mind usually just switches into "go and accomplish" mode, without necessarily always thinking of the most efficient *way* of accomplishing something.

Journalist Jessica Greene says in a *Fast Company* article, "Efficiency is about being productive with less effort."[4] Now that is something I can get behind. If I can have my cake and eat it too, I'm all in. It's like getting a mani and a pedi at the same time, listening to an audiobook while working out, or sipping cocktails while in the pool. It's called *efficiency*, and I'm here for it.

Focusing on productivity just makes us want to do even more in the same amount of time, jamming in as many tasks and as much impact as possible, and it leads to more wrinkles, gray hair, and exhaustion. But efficiency is about being productive in a way that won't burn us out in the long run and leaves us feeling content, well-rested, with a manageable workload, and, dare I say, even joyous.[5] And considering we're already good at running ourselves into the ground, focusing on efficiency is key to pulling ourselves out of the Type A Trap. When faced with a new project or task, ask yourself, *Is there a better way to do this?* The answer is almost always, *Yes!* Can you automate it? Delegate it? If you stopped doing it altogether, would it even matter?

Looking at how we do things critically and removing or streamlining steps and processes frees up more time for us to rest and reflect between tasks. More importantly, it frees up time for us to actually pursue the things that are important to us—whether that's working on your side hustle, date nights with your partner, or more time yelling a little too loudly on the sidelines of your kid's soccer game.

Psyched!

Dr. Darria Long

"The Do it All Discrepancy is the difference between how much a woman feels she needs to be able to do and what she actually can do. In our study, 82 percent of participants say they feel like they should be able to do it all, yet only 7 percent felt that they actually could do all that they needed to do. This discrepancy is directly tied to burnout. To decrease burnout, you have to decrease your demands. YOU get to choose what ALL is to you. And your ALL may be entirely different than what ALL is to someone else."

A second concept to consider when working on not doing it all is that you don't have to master everything on your own. I get it, we're overachievers. We like to take on new challenges just to see if we can do them. I've picked up tennis again after playing for a few years as a kid and trust me when I say it is *humbling*. But you better believe that the sporty achiever in me is on the court twice a week hammering balls into the net, over the fence, and over the line. I'm channeling my inner Serena and determined to get to the point where I can at least have a rally that lasts longer than two hits. When we're in leadership positions, we also know that people look up to us and expect us to have the answers. This can lead us to poring over data, reading countless books and articles, going down Google research rabbit holes, and generally inundating ourselves with information on whatever topic we need to know about at that time.

But here's the thing, there's another way. You don't have to go it alone. In case you haven't noticed, people LOVE talking about themselves. So let them. Ask for help, seek out experts in fields you're less certain about, make people feel needed and important and that their expertise is helping you out. Tapping others for information can free up your time to remain in your expert lane and not burn out your mental capacities by trying to master everything.

Trap Talk

Retired Navy SEAL Captain Chris Lindsay often speaks of the loneliness of command and high achievement. The higher up you go in any organization, public or private, the lonelier it can feel. You're the one whom everyone looks to for answers, but often, you're navigating uncharted waters and don't have anyone with you to consult. Many executives and CEOs feel alone. You need a truth-sayer, a right-hand person, a confidant—someone you really trust whom you can talk to. This could be anything from a stellar executive assistant or COO to a former boss or family member. As Captain Lindsay knows all too well, isolation is dangerous— both in combat and at home. If no one knows what's going on in your life, that's when problems occur. As high-level leaders, we need to know when to ask for help. We cannot expect to make good decisions in a perpetual vacuum. Yes, we may be in charge of the team, but we can't possibly know everything. By surrounding ourselves with trusted confidants and calling on them for help, we allow ourselves to not have to master everything. We can decode our flow and lean on them for insight in areas we aren't as knowledgeable about and, ultimately, make better decisions, feel less alone, and focus on the areas that light us up.

When I was at one of the lowest points in my burnout, but simultaneously one of the highest points in my career as the VP of marketing for the nation's largest healthcare staffing company, my boss was on my case like you couldn't believe. It felt like everything I did and said was wrong. One area he was particularly upset about was our digital ads. We had been running the same ads for a while, and it was time to refresh them. My team and I worked on a few new concepts but none of them hit the mark for him. After many phone calls that left me quietly sobbing on the other end without him knowing, it seemed like he was offended that I would even waste his time showing them to him, and I was wondering if he was seriously questioning my ability to run his marketing department. What he didn't know was that I was taking his phone calls while in the waiting room of an IVF clinic in Sacramento or at the kitchen table of my friend's place where we were staying during this process. I was smack in the middle of our third round of IVF, taking multiple shots daily, going to constant appointments, and trying desperately to keep my stress levels down to hopefully have a successful round, but to no avail.

Now I don't know about you, but when I'm feeling beat up, with an empty well and burned out, I'm not exactly at my creative peak. I've worked in advertising, marketing, and creative industries my whole career, but I couldn't come up with a good ad if my life depended on it during this time. My mind was numb. I was practically catatonic. It's no wonder my boss eventually got so frustrated with me that he called me up and asked me if I wanted to resign. The reality was, *I did want to resign!* I wanted to quit and spend my days lying on a beach in Tahiti, but alas, I needed the money and was by no means ready or able to quit.

One thing that helped me immensely during this terrible time was building out my team and hiring to my weaknesses and the areas my boss seemed most upset about. Our company had grown exponentially over the years, from a $100 million company when I started to a multi-billion-dollar company at the time of my burnout, but my marketing department was constantly under-resourced compared to other departments and the size of our company. When I finally secured additional head count, I focused my hiring to my weaknesses, dislikes, and the areas where I had the most friction with my boss. Two hires in particular were game-changers for me. I hired a director of database marketing and analytics as well as a creative director—both of which were experts in their fields and made my work life infinitely better the second they arrived.

By being truly honest with myself and taking the time to decode my flow and establish what I liked, what I was good at, where I liked to spend my time, what my team needed, and what the business needed, I was able to see that I needed help. I'd been so used to being in the trenches, fighting the good fight, that it was hard for me to realize that my role had grown, and I needed to get out of the trenches and into a more strategic role. I couldn't continue to work in the weeds and expect the team to thrive or my boss to be happy. I wasn't working efficiently, and I needed to find a better way.

Get Shifting Now

Create Your Personal Board of Directors

For as long as I can remember, I've been developing my own personal board of directors. I didn't realize I was doing it at the time, but I've collected key people in my life over the years who are experts on particular subjects, who care about me, and whom I can call on and ask for help at any time. And call on them I have! They have been there to talk me through new jobs, problems, and major life decisions.

Jeff Berger, the founder and CEO of Talent Inc., a career services firm, explores this concept in detail. He argues that most people begin their careers with the expectation they'll instantly find someone who will provide them with sage advice and help them navigate their careers. But the truth is, almost half of Americans say they've never had a professional mentor.[6]

I'm sure we can all agree that as much as we'd like it, we don't have incredible people banging on our door asking to be our mentor. And as we all know, it can be lonely out there flailing our way through new territory, including your first management or executive leadership position, marriage, kids, investing, navigating your first global pandemic, you name it.

So instead of going it alone, Berger recommends decoding your flow by creating a personal board of directors to help you navigate the uncharted waters of life. I started doing this years ago, using my brilliant cousin as the financial guru on my board. He never went to college but has always been amazing at making money. He's a self-made multimillionaire who owns hundreds of properties and always has his finger on the pulse of the economy. His stock advice alone has helped me grow my portfolio by over 50 percent.

Psyched!
Dr. Madelyn Blair

"Making decisions is an emotional activity even when you think it is logical. That said, emotions can hijack thinking. They are designed to do so. Having a personal board of directors that you can call on to assist you is like having others who may not be as emotionally connected with your concerns as you or may have different emotions in relation to them. Their perceptions can help you see beyond your own emotional attachments. At the same time, they are likely to become your social support. And every human being needs some social support. We are designed that way."

My former editor at *Orange Coast* magazine has been my writing mentor and like a second mom to me for nearly two decades now. When I started writing for her, I had no idea what I was doing. (One could argue I still don't, but that's another story). Through the wrath of her red pen, she slowly and painstakingly taught me how to write for magazines, how to interview people, how to show not tell, and everything else that comes with producing a monthly magazine. I continue to lean on her and look to her for advice on all things writing related.

My father has also been a pivotal member of my board. It's safe to call him the chairman of my board of directors. He is the most brilliant, yet humble, man you'll ever meet. He came from no money and lost his father at fifteen. He went on to get a full scholarship to UC Berkeley for undergrad, then he got a master's from UC Berkeley, another masters from UC Davis, and a PhD from

Harvard. He served in the navy and retired as a captain and went on to have an incredible career in defense and environmental engineering, then consulting for the likes of the United Nations, the World Bank, and the Asian Development Bank. He then taught at several universities, culminating in serving as the dean of the executive business school at Loyola Marymount University in Los Angeles before he finally retired.

His diverse background and level head have provided me with so much insight and counsel over the years. I can't even estimate the hours of time we've spent talking about my career, decisions, management issues, and more. He is my most trusted advisor, and I hope he lives forever.

Now, I realize not everyone is as lucky as me to have this type of relationship with their father. I know that I won the lottery on that front, and I don't ever take it for granted. But just because you may not have been blessed with the world's greatest father, that doesn't mean that you can't still build a kick-ass personal board of directors.

Trap Talk

Nick Rimedio, the general manager of the W Hotel in Hollywood, understands the importance of having a personal board of directors well. He says he's benefited from amazing mentors over the years and still speaks to them regularly. His personal board of directors is comprised of his closest, most trusted friends, confidants, and family. Nick says it's easiest for the Type A personalities to form a personal board of directors because they're already a trusted confidant to others and usually surround themselves with other similar, driven, motivated, accomplished personalities. Take a look at your people. It is likely you have boundless knowledge, sound advice, and trusted companions waiting to chat with you about life's possibilities.

To create your board, view yourself as a business developing a diverse board of advisers who are invested in your success, who can hold you accountable and help you out through the different stages of life.

Remember, you're creating an informal board. You're not actually going to hold board meetings or officially invite people to join. That would just be awkward. Instead, you'll cultivate your board by asking an individual what they think about a certain situation or problem you're facing. Over time, your personal board of advisors will be a small handful of mentors who will be able to give you advice on your career, family, finances, fitness, or any other topic you want to focus on. These people will not only help you navigate your way out of burnout if you find yourself stuck, but they're also incredible resources to check in with before you burn out to avoid it entirely.

Here's one thing to keep in mind though: if you don't have someone who fits the bill for one of these categories just yet, no problem. Find your favorite mentor online and absorb their teachings. Look to their work and thought leadership when you want to make a decision. So yes, Warren Buffett could be your financial advisor, Sara Blakely, the founder of Spanx, your business coach, or those hot twin property guys could be your real estate gurus until you gain those advisors in your actual network.

The point is you don't have to master everything yourself. When you focus on maintaining a small group of advisors, you'll reap the benefits of their professional guidance throughout your life so you can focus on the items that truly bring you joy.

Practice the Love It or Leave It Test

One simple tactic I've found useful to help you decode your day-to-day flow is the Love It or Leave It test. Here's how it works: Do a task for seven minutes. After seven minutes, decide whether to love it (continue on with the task) or leave it (abort mission). If you repeatedly find yourself changing tasks after seven minutes and putting off the same task again and again, find a way to delegate that task so you can spend more time doing what you love and leave the rest.

Trap Talk

Ben Nemtin, star of MTV's *The Buried Life*, number one *New York Times*–bestselling author, and speaker talks about how his overactive and pressurized subconscious constantly drives him and makes him not settle for less than perfection, when in reality no one else would notice. At times, Ben admits to falling into the Type A Trap. It has hindered him developing a healthy life balance and contributed to depression and anxiety. He feels he doesn't always celebrate his wins and is always looking at the next thing and not slowing down. It's taken practice, but he strives to find the middle ground and states that, "When you're creating things at the highest level, being graceful with yourself and being able to let things go is key."

After some trial and error, I now use the Love It or Leave It Test constantly throughout my life. When my husband and I first moved in together, I knew cleaning would be an issue. I like everything put away and a clean house. He seems to not notice if there is dust and crumbs everywhere and wouldn't change the sheets or towels for weeks if left to his own devices. After doing all the cleaning for the first few months, hating it, and getting resentful, I realized I didn't love it, so I needed to leave it. I hired a cleaner to come twice a month, trimmed the budget in other areas to afford it, and now the house is clean, we don't bicker about it, and I can spend more time doing things I love.

Psyched!
Dr. Marsha Chinichian

"There is a significant body of research that supports this mindset shift philosophy. Focusing on your strengths can lead to greater success, happiness, and fulfillment in both your personal and professional life, which means you'll be less likely to burn out. By having clarity on your strengths, you can assess how often you rely on them each day and if your job and responsibilities align with them often enough. Our weaknesses are for someone else to flourish in."[7]

Let Me Think about It. "No!"

As Warren Buffett says, "The difference between successful people and really successful people is that really successful people say no to almost everything."[8] And if the Oracle of Omaha says it, then it must be true! Similar to the productivity-over-efficiency principle, Buffett argues that busy people are driven by doing more, so they often let their egos get in the way, keep saying yes even though it's not sustainable, and eventually crash and burn.

In order to decode our flow, we have to know when to say no and mean it. Sometimes saying no can mean not pursuing an amazing opportunity because you know deep down inside that it's not going to serve you in the long term. This is why people talk about vision boarding and goal setting so much. It's not just woo-woo nonsense. If you don't know where you're heading, how will you know when you get there? Once you decode your flow and really have a clear understanding of where you want to go and what your priorities and goals are, it's so much easier to say no to things that don't help you get closer to that goal. But when you have no idea where you are headed, that's when you get sucked into saying yes to all sorts of garbage.

Ben Nemtin warns, "Be careful of what's driving you. Is it you or are you trying to impress other people?" It's far too easy to let our egos and social media likes drive our behavior. Then, before we know it, we're pursuing someone else's dream or someone else's vision of our life instead of our own. When you have a clear vision of your hopes, dreams, and passions, it's much easier to say no to anything that doesn't align. I know far too many people who have become doctors and lawyers because their parents wanted them to, only to find themselves miserable, in debt up to their eyeballs, and feeling trapped years later. It's not worth it. Say no now and be happy sooner.

You have to be personally connected and driven to do something, otherwise you won't perform at your best. In short, say no to what doesn't align with you and let the rest of that shit go.

First Things First

You know whether you're a morning person or not. Whether you do your best work after a run, after your second cup of coffee, or late at night when the house is finally quiet and you get some alone time. Whatever your prime time looks like, make sure you use it to do your most important work. It can be tempting to do the small quick-win type of work first. And yes, while it's important to feel like you're making progress with quick wins, often those simple tasks are the easiest, and you could do them when you're tired or not as engaged.

When your mind is sharpest, that's when to put all the other crap aside and dig deep into the work that will get you where you want to go. This could be writing that business proposal, crafting your website copy, putting together that sales deck, strategizing and planning for your team's quarterly goals, or any number of other items that take the most concentration and work.

What this doesn't look like is cleaning up, filing, scrolling Instagram, or researching (if you only knew how much time I've spent "researching" and telling myself that I was doing something productive). All of these little, mindless tasks take up so much of our time. You don't think they do, but then over time, hours pass, and you still haven't done any of the real work you need to do—the work that's going to move you closer to your goals, hopes, and dreams.

Gary Keller and Jay Papasan call this focusing on "the one thing" in their book by the same name.[9] They argue that the narrower you keep the scope of your work, the more likely you are to really succeed. When we stretch ourselves thin and try to do too many things at once, we water down our productivity. By ignoring all the things you could do and focusing on the most important thing that will get you closer to your dream, you have a much higher chance of achieving extraordinary results.

Trap Talk

Bobbie Singh-Allen, mayor of Elk Grove, California, a suburb of Sacramento, this principle into action every day. After a life of serial Type A-ism, she has finally realized that she doesn't have to do it all. She knows that if she wants to do something important, she needs to prioritize it. She looks at her calendar and constantly assesses whether she's spending her time in areas that are important to her or not. If she hasn't sat down and had dinner with her family or watched a movie with her husband in a while, she reassesses and redirects her energy to her priorities.

For me, this looks like getting up at 5:00 a.m. to write. I am a morning person through and through. I struggle to keep my eyes open after it's dark, go to bed early, and always get up early. It's when I'm most alert, energized, fired up, and ready to tackle the day and any big projects I'm working on.

Before I quit my corporate job, I always liked to have some sort of side hustle. I love creating something out of nothing and having multiple income streams. But in order to get the work done for my side hustles, I needed to get up early to do them. After years of sleeping in later, working my day job, and then coming home exhausted only to have dinner, go to bed, and do it all over again the next day, I got resentful. Resentful that all I was doing with every waking hour was working for someone else. I never had the time or energy to work on my own projects.

Once I started getting up earlier to write and working on my passion projects, everything changed. Going from getting up at 7:00 a.m. to getting up at 5:00 a.m. is a bit of a shock to the system. Instead of making that jump all at once, I started by getting up thirty minutes earlier. Those extra thirty minutes didn't affect me very much sleep-wise, but they also didn't give me much time to work on my side hustle. So after a week, I got up an hour earlier than before. Over the course of a few weeks, I worked my way up to getting up at 5:00 a.m. This allowed me plenty of time to wake up, make coffee, get to my desk, and really dig in for an extended period of time. I eventually got to the point where I worked on my projects from 5:00 a.m. to 7:30 a.m., then worked out (a few days a week), got ready for work, and started my day job. After work, when I was tired, I could just relax, because I knew I'd already accomplished two and a half hours of work on my personal projects.

I felt fulfilled, my projects moved forward, I devoted the time when my mind was sharpest to my own projects, and I felt like I had a nice balance of personal projects and day job. I use the same thinking when I work out at the gym. In general, I'm more of a yoga, Pilates, and tennis girl. I hate doing cardio. But I know it's important to get the blood flowing, your heart pounding, and the sweat pouring. So any time I go to an actual gym, I always start with fifteen minutes of cardio. I tell myself I only have to do fifteen minutes, then I can do whatever I want. By getting the hardest, most laborious part over with first, I can then spend the rest of my workout taking my time doing the exercises that are more enjoyable for me.

Any way you slice it, whatever work is on your plate, find the time when you're at your mental and energetic peak, and do your hardest, most important tasks at that time. You'll not only accomplish more, but you'll feel good about putting your best energy into the tasks, projects, and people that are most important to you and your long-term happiness.

• • •

Decoding your flow in both your personal and professional life is the essential first step in creating positive changes to help you beat burnout and sustain peak performance. The key is to shift your mindset from feeling the need to master everything no matter what to practicing strict and methodical selection of how you spend your time.

When we get clear on our life and career goals, it's easier to see how the inefficiencies that pop up and annoy us are clues that we need to decode our flow. Similarly, trying to be all things to all people never results in our best work or mental health. When we realize we don't have to do it all and instead can call on others to help, we can focus our attention and energy on the things that help us thrive.

By becoming laser-focused on how we allocate our time every day—whether personally or professionally—we can decode our flow, reduce the noise, get rid of the obligations and tasks that feel like a long dental appointment, and focus on the things that really light us up.

Decode Your Flow Jumpstart

- **Start your personal board of directors.**
  Make a list of five people who could be a good fit for your personal board of directors. Think through the different important areas of your life that you would like guidance and insight in. This could be related to your career, finances, relationships, family, spirituality, mental health, physical health, fitness,

travel, hobbies, philanthropy, parenting, or any number of other areas. You don't need an expert in all of these areas though. Just pick a few that you feel are the most important to you and start your list. I always advise starting with the areas you're most passionate about. You may feel like you need the most work on your parenting, but if you're really passionate about exercise, start there. That's not to say becoming a better parent isn't important, it just means that we can't focus on everything at once. Start with the area that lights you up, as you're more likely to experience quick wins there. Those wins will then feed into the other areas of your life. Once you have your list, make a point to reach out to those five people just to check in and say hello in the next week. You could also share an article or book you just read that you think they'd enjoy, or just simply say you thought of them and felt like reaching out to say hello. The point is to start a dialogue. Once the conversations have started, make sure to keep up with them personally, and build the relationship by talking about more than just their field of expertise.

- **Practice Love It or Leave It.**
  As you go about your day today, pay attention to the tasks you complete. Often, we just glide through our day on auto-pilot and don't even realize when we're doing things that are misaligned with our long-term goals. Be cognizant of this today. With every task you do, give it seven minutes. If you love it, carry on. If you hate it, create a list of items you want to leave. Removing leave-it tasks from your weekly schedule can take some time and adjustments. Once you get a list of all the tasks you're ready to leave, then you can start coming

up with creative solutions for removing them. But if you don't even know what tasks they are, you can't address them. So get out that paper and start creating your leave-it list.

- **Say no today.**
  What can you say no to today? Look at your calendar, look at your emails, look at your to-do list. What's on there that you're doing out of obligation or because you feel like you should but you're really not passionate about? Those are the items that are ripe for a *big fat no!* Promise yourself that you'll say no to at least one thing that doesn't align with your priorities today. It's time to stop "should-ing" on yourself and start saying no to the things that take you further away from your truth and your joy.

- **Figure out what's first.**
  When during the day are you at your physical and mental peak? Block out thirty minutes during that time in your calendar. If you can't manage thirty, then start with fifteen minutes. Literally get your phone out right now and block out that time in your calendar every day for a week. Use that time to work on the most important tasks of the week. Rinse and repeat for the next four weeks. A month from now, take stock of how much progress you made on that important aspect of your life. Remember to continue assessing and assigning your most important tasks to that time block to continue this exponential growth!

- **Print out your mental health toolkit.**
  Print out my mental health toolkit at www.erinstafford. com/toolkit. Put it somewhere you can see it daily. Tape it to

your desk or bathroom or closet mirror. Pin it to your bulletin board or make it your desktop image. Get creative. The point is to keep it visible and easy to refer to at all times. Any time you feel overwhelmed or flustered, take a look at the sheet and implement one of the many simple solutions to help you keep burnout at bay.

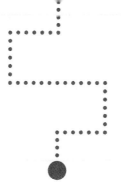

RELEASE THE REINS

Instead of micromanaging and controlling everything,
shift to empowering others to drive longevity.

Many peak performers find it difficult to delegate and relinquish control. One could say we're control freaks. I mean, I've heard it said, maybe that's you. *But obviously, that's not me.*

Maybe you insist on leading every meeting or planning every team event. Perhaps you're the person who requires every single project, regardless of size, to have your approval before it moves forward. I know I've been guilty of that at times. Or maybe you're the parent who absolutely loses it when your partner makes spur-of-the-moment plans with your kids. You may be the person who insists on being copied on every email your team sends, just so you can "have visibility." Maybe you're the girl who demanded she plan her own wedding shower and bachelorette weekend, because you know no one could possibly plan it as seamlessly as you.

The reality is when you're a high achiever, you will constantly be working your way through transition periods in life. Change is the one constant we can count on in this lifetime, and often during periods of change, we find ourselves holding on even tighter than we usually do—sometimes onto things that aren't serving us or our dreams.

The transitions from doer to manager, from solopreneur to CEO, from single thirtysomething to married parent, from adventurous undergrad to stressed graduate student all test us—the countless minor and major transitions we go through are all challenging in their own ways. No matter what industry you work in or what your role is in your personal or professional relationships, when we grow . . . it's difficult. These seasons require us to look at our time, energy, and values differently. Those parts of us need to grow with us. When we level up, sometimes we need to leave aspects of those old roles behind.

But even when we know deep down we need to let go . . . we just can't. I know I've certainly held on to tasks too long just to make myself feel needed. In my previous role, I required all creative to be approved by me long after I had an incredible creative director whom I trusted could do it. I insisted on reviewing every piece of collateral that went out even though I had teams of people who were fully qualified to review them. And every photo needed my approval as well. On the one hand, I felt like I was the last line of defense in case something was wrong, but on the other hand, I know I was just slowing down the process of an efficient marketing department and sometimes hindering the growth of people who reported to me.

I also hold onto things for too long in my personal life. Like when being a back-seat driver infuriates my husband, yet I keep doing it because clearly my way would be faster! Or when I get frustrated that I'm the one who makes all the plans for my family, but then also get mad when someone else makes the plans because they don't do it to my liking. I know I need to let these things go, but it's hard.

This shift in perspective can jostle our need for control. In order to embrace our new roles, sometimes others have to step in and take over where we've stepped away. We can question ourselves and our value and often might think, *I should be able to do it all.* And when we don't have this control—or quite frankly the energy—our fear spikes. I know I've felt like that before. And it means I've held on for far too long to tasks that no longer serve me, my life, or my career.

That's why the second mindset shift is to ***release the reins.*** To prevent burnout, escape the Type A Trap, and sustain peak performance, we need to let go of micromanaging and controlling everything and focus more on empowering others to drive longevity! Because when we empower others and remove items from our plate, we also empower ourselves to stay committed to the things that truly light us up and bring us fulfillment.

Talking Shift

I know releasing your hold over things you care about is difficult. When you're the one ultimately responsible for something, it's hard to delegate the task to someone else. Type A people care deeply about their commitments, and releasing control to allow others to try and sometimes fail can feel counterintuitive. In some cases, such as becoming a manager, when people make mistakes, we're still affected. Releasing this need for control is hard, especially if you have a hard-to-please boss.

As a leader, you've probably gotten ahead by excelling at your job. But many of us haven't received much formal management training. Maybe you've been promoted and promoted, and the next thing you know, you're managing a team at the same time you're trying to figure out how to be a manager and what's expected of you. It may feel shaky at first, but as high achievers we always find a way.

If you're anything like me, you listen to podcasts and read books by great leaders, seek out leadership keynote speakers, attend conferences, and hope for the best. We also meticulously review and consider our own performance on a regular basis. But once you're out of the trenches and leading a team, how do you make sure your boss knows you're still working and doing things when you now have people to do them for you? And if you let go, how do you cope with feeling like suddenly you no longer have control over the direction of your career or life? This sense of control that we hold onto so fiercely makes us feel like we can predict things that may take us for a loop later, and as Type As, we like to be prepared. What we often don't realize until it is too late, though, is this death grip on control leads to unnecessary stress, strain on relationships, and complex mental health issues.

This need for control is something I still think about constantly. The transition from manager to leader is one that doesn't come easy to everyone. We hold on for dear life to the things we've always been successful at, so we feel like we're still adding value. But this just feeds burnout and falling into the Type A Trap. We also need to learn that our inherent value does not come from our productivity.

Ultimately, when your team is happy and performing at a high level, you're doing your job well. And if you're not getting any feedback from your boss, you're doing your job. No news is good news. But that transition can be a doozy. That's why it's important we learn how to release the reins and understand that by letting go, we're actually empowering others, doing our job as leaders, and, ultimately, preserving our own sanity, avoiding the Type A Trap, and preventing burnout in the process.

It is important to note there's a difference between *delegating* and *abdicating*. Understanding the difference between the two is imperative, especially in business settings. A lot of new managers may think they're delegating tasks, projects, or responsibilities, but in fact they are abdicating. They simply hand off the tasks with little to no involvement, follow-up, or guidance. As a manager, it is your job to set your team up for success. Delegate the necessary responsibilities and tasks to facilitate your transition, but give your team the context, direction, expectations, deadlines, and support they need to accomplish them successfully. Simply delegating a task to a team member and then never thinking about it again is abdicating. Ultimately, you as the manager are responsible for your team's projects, so if the team doesn't do, complete, or lead them correctly, it's on *you*. That's why it's important to understand how to release the reins in a way that takes work off your plate, but still accomplishes your goals successfully and honors your duties to mentor and coach others.

Delegate or Die, It's That Simple

I realize this section title sounds a little dramatic, but it's true. In life, no matter if it is professional or personal—you're either growing or you're dying. When it's time to scale opportunities or existing businesses, releasing the reins is *essential*. You can't support growth without learning how to delegate certain things as a leader. And without delegating, you'll end up killing your business or yourself through burnout in the long run. Let's avoid both of those, please! Choose delegation. Choose growth.

When I was in my early thirties, I had a jewelry line I designed and made myself. It had a beachy, bohemian vibe and was growing steadily. I bootstrapped everything and was getting to the point where I couldn't grow faster unless I hired someone to help. But being the Type A control freak that I am, I felt like no one could possibly understand my aesthetic and brand as much as me. I worried that if I delegated any of the production or marketing that the brand and in turn, my sales, would suffer.

I couldn't have been more wrong. I was introduced to a friend of a friend who had the most fabulous personal style, aesthetic, and Instagram feed; worked in marketing already; and was looking for extra work. I hired her to help me for a few hours each week. With what, I didn't know at the time. I just knew I needed help.

She ended up doing all sorts of different things for me—responding to social media comments, curating and creating marketing emails, art directing photos shoots, and more. She was a godsend and ultimately helped me double my store count and social media followers and increase online sales. I wouldn't have been able to do any of that without releasing the reins and trusting that she would be able to help me and my budding brand grow.

When Julie Rice and Elizabeth Cutler founded SoulCycle, the high-end cycling gym chain, in 2006, they only had to manage themselves. Today, the company leads more than 700 employees. In order to sustain and expand their success, they've had to release the reins on their rapidly growing business and let their employees pick up more of the work over time. Like many of us, Julie and Elizabeth struggled with the transition from entrepreneurs to leaders of a growing company. They were in the trenches doing everything themselves, then they had to adjust to being leaders who were delegating and growing new leaders who report to them. This shift was imperative so they could focus on scaling their business and managing their company's vision at a higher level. But this shift was also difficult. They thought that if they didn't touch every aspect of their business that it would be done wrong. Sound familiar?

For them, culture was the key to releasing the reins. By doubling down on their company culture—making sure they hired people "who really understood the DNA of their business and what they were trying to accomplish"—they were able to let go and trust that decisions would be made that reflected the culture and direction of their vision for SoulCycle. Once they released the reins, they were able to triple their number of locations in a fraction of the time it used to take to open them.[1]

Trap Talk

Keith Karwelies, a former music industry executive and current nurse leader, was on the frontlines fighting COVID-19 in New York City. He understands burnout and the fear of releasing the reins all too well. In his vocation, one wrong decision can literally mean life or death. "My fear of not having it go well if I wasn't involved was what led to my burnout," he said. "I trust my team, but do I trust them without me present? That's how we burn out. We need to trust others to take on those roles." After working around the clock in a high-stakes, high-pressure environment for years during the pandemic, he's finally starting to take the steps needed to release the reins and empower his team. He has perfected delegation: "You're never going to be satisfied with the outcome if you don't empower and train people to do it better. The passing of the reins has to be redefined as 'I'm not handing you the reins, but I'm going to help motivate you or mentor you so that I have confidence in your process.'"

Let Go to Grow

Sarah Kauss, founder of the popular water bottle brand S'well, found herself in a similar boat. After growing her company to more than one hundred employees, she was so inundated with the day-to-day operations of running the organization that she didn't have time to focus on other opportunities for growth—both for S'well and in her personal life.[2]

Things like sustainability—the issue that got her started in the first place—were becoming huge drivers for her customers, yet she felt she was pulled in so many operational directions that she couldn't do what she did best. She knew there was so much more she could do, and she realized she needed to release the reins. It was time to find a CEO to replace her. They would take over the day-to-day running of the business and help it grow so she could focus on global innovation, brand vision, partnerships, and other high-level initiatives.[3]

Sarah knew that in order for her to fully release the reins and prevent her from micromanaging, she needed a CEO who had been one multiple times before. She needed someone who could hit the ground running, someone whom she could trust and who had the depth of experience from previous engagements to make sound decisions for her company. With no one internally who fit the bill, she hired an executive search firm, but she ultimately found her new CEO through her own social network.

With the new CEO on board, Sarah said she could finally stop living in a constant state of worry and burnout. She knows that she's released the reins to the right person and is looking forward to a vacation that doesn't involve a conference badge for once.[4]

Psyched!
Dr. Marsha Chinichian

"Let go of perfectionism. Accepting that things may not always go according to plan can help managers avoid micromanaging. Does your anxiety kick up when letting go of things you can't control? That's not sustainable for your well-being and health. Research suggests that a large percentage of our worries may be unfounded . . . A study conducted by Penn State University found that 85 percent of the things people worry about never actually happen and that people's ability to cope with difficult situations is much better than they expect."

Like Sarah Kauss, founder and CEO of Stitch Fix, Katrina Lake, knew it was time to release the reins after a decade at the helm of her company.[5] Stitch Fix is an e-commerce clothing site that helps you pick out clothes through fine-tuned algorithms and personal stylists. Katrina's been celebrated as one of the most influential tech CEOs, and in 2017 she was the youngest female CEO to take a company public. Yet she knew it was time for a change.

After selling $7 billion worth of clothes over the years, she'd figured that part out. She craved time to focus on issues that aligned with her core business but that also lit up her entrepreneurial spirit again, such as sustainability and social impact. Katrina wanted to focus her time on initiatives like reselling used items, garment recycling, and even milling and sewing new clothing from recycled fibers at her company's facility in Pennsylvania.

So, she passed the baton to Elizabeth Spaulding in one of the very few female-to-female transitions of power in a public company.[6] At that time, Spaulding had already been Stitch Fix's president for a couple of years, so she deeply understood the purpose, culture, and operational details of the company. It was natural for her to take over as CEO, and because she already knew the company so well, it gave Katrina a sense of peace knowing she was leaving the company she'd worked so hard to create in good hands. But she didn't go far—she stayed on as chairperson of the board where she could continue to monitor and influence direction without getting bogged down in the day-to-day operations.

After releasing the reins and empowering a new CEO, Katrina escaped the Type A Trap and the ongoing burnout cycle she found herself in and can now focus on making Stitch Fix a leader in sustainability—something that's not only meaningful for the company and shareholders but also for the planet.

Aytekin Tank, the founder and CEO of online form builder Jotform, discovered the importance of releasing the reins when he and his wife were expecting their second child.[7] He desperately wanted to take paternity leave to spend those first few precious months bonding with his baby and helping his wife while she recovered, but the mental distress it caused him thinking about his company imploding without him around was debilitating. He knew he had to release the reins to make it happen. In order to take a full three-month paternity leave that allowed him the time and space to connect with his family and not facilitate a work-from-home situation, he trained a portion of his employees to take over his job completely while he was away.

Aytekin started preparing his company early in his wife's pregnancy. He reviewed his daily tasks and figured out what could be delegated or automated. Since they were a relatively small company, he realized he oversaw a bunch of random tasks, simply because they didn't fit anyone else's job description. He delegated those, trained employees one-on-one, and made sure expectations were clear. He watched how people performed his tasks and was there to offer help and advice as needed. Like the SoulCycle founders, he also made sure that the company's vision and future plans were known to everyone to ensure they were headed in the right direction while he was away.

The result of all Aytekin's planning? He took his full leave and realized that he'd been holding onto certain tasks out of habit. He had organized his release of the reins for a specific season of his life, but he realized the practice had a far greater impact on his ability to lead. Instead of employees screwing things up while he was away like he feared, he found most of the tasks were done better by others because they had more time to focus on them, where he was always stretched so thin.

Releasing the reins and taking a leave of absence not only helped Aytekin connect with his newborn and toddler, but it also demonstrated his commitment to maintaining a work-life balance to his employees—something he believes is important to model and not just pay lip service to.

Delegating . . . the Right Way

As I mentioned earlier in this chapter, there's a huge difference between delegation and abdication. Learning how to do the former without doing the latter takes skill and practice. As a manager and leader, you don't want to be seen as a micromanager, but you cannot simply abdicate all responsibility and call it releasing the reins. That just leads to chaos, confusion, and disappointment all around. Many founders and new managers resist delegating because they feel like it ends up taking more time, and it would just be easier to do things themselves. That's because, as Alisa Cohn writes in her *Inc.* article, most people aren't delegating *correctly*.[8]

There are three key questions Cohn advocates asking when delegating to ensure you're setting your team (and yourself) up for success:

How much experience does your employee have?

Every seasoned leader understands the frustration of asking an employee to do a project only to get the finished product back and have it look nothing like what you hoped for or expected. Conversations are had, frustration abounds on both sides, and ultimately the project needs to be redone and the deadline is missed.

Most of the time, Cohn argues, the reason for the misalignment is because the leader asks a more junior person to do the task but treats them as if they were a senior executive—only giving them a high-level framework but not walking them through exactly what they had in mind or giving them the opportunity to ask questions. The junior person is excited to get the project, is usually too embarrassed to ask too many questions, and, ultimately because of their inexperience, doesn't even know what questions to ask anyway.

If you've studied Ken Blanchard's course on situational leadership, as many leaders have, this will sound very similar. As leaders, we need to ask ourselves what skill set our team has and then release the reins and manage to their level accordingly when delegating.

What does "done" look like?

Failing to align on what "done" looks like with your team member when delegating can lead to unnecessary confusion and frustration. You may have an idea in your head, but if you don't communicate it, your employee will come back with something completely different. You'll go back and forth, and they'll ultimately need to redo it. Being crystal clear on what the finished product should look like and aligning expectations at the beginning, especially when delegating to a more junior person, may take longer at the beginning, but will save time and frustration on both sides in the long run.

What is the deadline?

Too often, leaders delegate tasks and projects without setting a clear deadline. They're then left having to regularly ask for status updates and when the project will be completed. This means they aren't truly able to cross this off their list—which is the whole point of delegating in the first place! Leaders may feel that the deadline is assumed, and some new managers might not want to appear pushy. But setting clear expectations and deadlines upfront will reduce your stress as a leader and allow your team to work steadily toward a specific goal.

Psyched!
Dr. Madelyn Blair

"To release the reins, you need to bring staff to where they actually see *your* vision—see it so well they catch the fire of what you are trying to do. This is a skill that can be developed by any leader. It's called *storytelling*. It begins with you understanding your own story, then developing that story into something that a listener can't help but see as you tell it. When they see it clearly, they begin to tell the story themselves. At this point, you can trust them to work toward making that story a reality. Releasing is all about trust—in your staff and in yourself."

Delegation is never easy, but it's necessary to avoid falling into the Type A Trap and burning out. By implementing these simple questions and tactics, new managers and seasoned leaders alike can become better delegators, not abdicators, empower their teams, and ultimately drive their own longevity as peak performers and successful leaders.

Get Shifting Now

Let Others Own It

In group settings, allowing others to take ownership of responsibilities facilitates loyalty and stronger connections to core missions, making everyone more successful in the long run. Giving others ownership—literally or figuratively—allows leaders to release the reins and helps prevent the inevitable cycle of relentless burnout and ultimately falling into the Type A Trap.

Team members like to feel like they're in charge of something, even small, less strategic or impactful tasks. When I was VP of marketing and looked after conferences (among a million other things), my director of conferences and I gave the responsibility of keeping track of all our swag (inventory, ordering, shipping out) to a new conference assistant. It isn't a difficult task, but it does require attention to detail and being proactive to make sure we don't run out of items. She loved it. Since she was young and early in her career, she wasn't in charge of particular conferences yet. Giving her this task allowed her to feel like we trusted her, that her role was valuable, and that she had clear ownership of something.

I had another team member who was itching for a promotion and more responsibility. Unfortunately, at the time we didn't have a role for him to move into, but we slowly made him in charge of leading Zoom meetings. Once he got the hang of that, we asked him to manage a small web design project—this included wrangling members from multiple departments and simultaneously gave him exposure to those departments. He did such a great job and really stepped up that we ultimately moved him into a project manager role where his personality and all the previous experience he had managing calls and small projects could shine.

Is there a small, seemingly simple task you can offload onto someone more junior? You'll get it off your plate, and they'll feel like their responsibility is increasing. It's a win-win. You may have heard of employee-owned companies, one of the most popular being REI, the iconic outdoor adventure outfitter. The official term is ESOP (employee stock ownership plan), but the concept is simple: employees are all owners of the company, therefore the CEO works for them. Employees have a say in decision-making and feel connected to the company, its profits, and productivity on a deep level because it affects their bottom line.

New Belgium Brewing, the company behind Fat Tire and other popular beers, is an ESOP.[9] They discovered early on the value of having employee buy-in on all levels. While it can definitely be frustrating and time consuming at times to gather feedback from everyone and build consensus, giving employees ownership ensures they aren't just clocking in and zoning out. They are constantly harnessing innovation and are on the lookout for process improvements and money-saving ideas.

These ideas can be simple, like when the shipping guy notices a lot of executives requesting beer samples to be sent overnight for one hundred dollars when they could be sent via three-day shipping for eight dollars. Most of the time it's not necessary for the beer to be at its destination the next day. This simple step saves the company hundreds of thousands of dollars a year, but likely would have been ignored if the shipping department didn't feel personally invested in the company.

These ideas can also be more complex. When the loading dock manager noticed a number of broken wood pallets arriving with the new kegs from their keg supplier—between twenty and fifty per week—he knew he could get a refund for them. The problem was, someone needed to log the broken pallets, and that was time consuming. But in doing so, the company could save at least fifty dollars per week—which is several hours of pay for most loading dock employees.[10] Because he now thinks holistically about all the parts of the company, the loading dock manager has an owner's mindset and is constantly looking for ways to improve things.

By giving employees actual ownership of the company through an ESOP, the CEO and leaders of New Belgium Brewing can release the reins a bit. They don't have to worry about every last detail of the company at all times, because they know their employees are constantly on the lookout for new and improved ways of doing things. They're invested, literally. This allows leaders to focus on other aspects of the company or other areas of their life they've been neglecting while simultaneously helping to create a company culture of shared responsibility.

But giving employees ownership of the company isn't the only way for them to feel empowered to make innovative suggestions that help the bottom line. Heineken Mexico, another global beer brand (can you tell happy hour is on my mind?), takes swift action on employee input. Implementing one simple suggestion from a maintenance worker is saving the company several millions of dollars a year while making a huge impact on sustainability and the planet.

Working daily with the waste coming out of the brewery, the maintenance worker noticed that more than half the trash from the breweries was the paper labels that had been removed from the old bottles.[11] Heineken had to pay for the paper to be shipped out, and it ultimately just ended up in landfills. A lose-lose situation for the company and the planet.

Because the maintenance worker felt ownership in his role and the company, he went to the CEO, Dolf van den Brink, with an idea:

Why not sell the used paper labels they were previously paying to send to landfills to paper companies to make napkins and tissues? The CEO was so pleased with the idea that he implemented it immediately. He also saw firsthand what organizations big or small are capable of when they can unleash the hidden passions and ideas of their employees.[12] He sums it up perfectly by saying, "A big part of humanity is suppressed in organizations and bureaucracies. But when you can find a way to tap into that, and appeal to people's passions and unleash their energies, amazing things can be done."[13]

Releasing the reins comes in many forms. From letting go of micromanaging and growing leaders under you to run the business so you can scale to empowering your team members to have ownership of the company—whether literally or figuratively—so they feel personally connected to the bottom line and constantly seek ways to improve it. Releasing the reins gives leaders the mental space to find balance in their lives and avoid falling into the Type A Trap. It allows us to not have to think of everything ourselves, to rely on others for innovative ideas, and empowers our teams to feel connected to our organizations' purpose and bottom line. Only through releasing the reins on all levels and empowering others can we truly find the balance we crave and avoid burnout for the long term.

Transition from Doer to Manager

As I mentioned earlier in this chapter, the transitions we encounter as we grow and embrace new opportunities can be real doozies. And when that transition happens in a hyper-growth organization, all bets are off. As the head of marketing for the largest healthcare staffing company in the country, my team grew from three people to more than sixty in the span of a couple years, and during the pandemic, our revenue grew exponentially. It was INSANE growth that no one is really ever prepared for. Everything changes in an instant, and there is no time to properly plan and prepare. This can lead to miscommunication, confusion, low team morale, unclear priorities, jumbled roles and responsibilities, decreased productivity, siloed departments, and more.[14]

There are many ways to manage growing pains. I could write a whole book on hyper-growth leadership. But one of the easiest and most effective ways to manage rapid growth on your team as a manager is to "give away your Legos," as the folks at Trello, the popular project management software, say. What do they mean by that? They mean giving away different pieces of your job.

But why would you want to do that? When starting your career or business, you use your own Legos. You build towers of work around you based on your natural skill set that often turn into full-blown cities. But when you start to scale your business or team and grow in your career, all of a sudden there are many other people around you building their own towers. Our initial instinct is to protect what's ours and hoard our Legos—those tasks and responsibilities that we feel deep ownership of.[15] But this scarcity mindset isn't sustainable and can lead to falling into the Type A Trap and ultimately burning out. It hinders us as individuals, but it also holds back the company's growth.

Instead, we need to give away our Legos. Share those tasks, projects, and responsibilities with others as your team grows. This does two things: it empowers new team members by giving them a chance to build something even better than you did and frees up your time to focus on inspiring and supporting your team as well as focusing on bigger, more strategic goals and projects. It also means trusting others to make good decisions about projects you care about. And when people feel trusted, they feel empowered and motivated. Ultimately, by transitioning from doer to manager and releasing the reins, you empower your team and drive longevity in your career as a leader and peak performer while simultaneously supporting your organization's growth. It's a win-win. So why is it so hard?

Trap Talk

Keith Karwelies, the nurse leader we heard from earlier, sums up the difficulty of transitioning from doer to manager perfectly by saying, "I know it won't be the same as me. I can't just say you're doing it wrong if I don't give you the help to get there. Empowering others makes your life easier and better at work. If you do it all, you'll burn out so fast." Keith describes that it took him time to learn how to coach and mentor his team as he began delegating, so he felt confident tasks were getting done correctly and safely and his team felt supported and empowered to do their jobs well and grow in the process.

Find Your Hype Group

One tactic that's helped me personally through this tricky transition from doer to manager is to find a hype group of like-minded people who are in similar chapters of their lives and career. Sometimes when we're moving up into leadership positions, we need others to remind us that we're capable. Unfortunately, if all your friends are at different stages of their lives, they aren't always the best people to help. For example, if all your friends are married with young kids and spend the time you have together talking about breast feeding, changing diapers, and day care, you aren't going to feel fulfilled when you really need someone to talk to you about management issues and how to delegate better.

I get it. Parenthood, especially new parenthood, is all consuming. It's a full-frontal assault, and I get that it's all one can think about during that season. But as someone who doesn't have kids yet, I often need connection with people at a different stage of their lives.

One way I've found groups of like-minded people is attending conferences or networking events. Things like women's conferences, chamber of commerce mixers, alumni association meetings for your college or university, young professionals' groups, women in business groups, or, if you can swing it financially, getting a business coach or joining a mastermind group can all help.

A lot of coaches and conferences have online communities you can join or private Facebook groups full of attendees or alumni of a certain event. These are incredible places to find motivated, driven people to connect with. They are usually looking for people just like you as well. So next time you're attending a conference or taking an online course, get active in the corresponding groups. You'll likely find your people, or even just one person you really connect with. Stay in touch with them. You won't regret it.

I've moved cities and countries many times. Every time I move, I have to recreate my network of people and friends from scratch. It's not easy, but it can be fun. You can reinvent yourself, redefine who you are and how you want to be perceived in the world, and be intentional with whom you spend your time with.

As Warren Buffett says, success relies on surrounding yourself with the right people.[16] You'll naturally move in the direction of the people you surround yourself with most, so it's important to find your people. People who inspire you, motivate you, encourage you, and make you a better version of yourself. People who are further along than you whom you can learn from and who can help you advance in your career and other areas of your life. If the people in your social circle aren't giving you energy, inspiring you, and lighting you up, it's time to find some new people.

Create Exhibition Matches

One simple tactic that helped the former presidential aide and diplomat that I interviewed release the reins is to create what he calls "exhibition matches"—opportunities for your team members to practice a task or skill with minimal risk to drive competency quickly. This allows team members to test out new skills and get help and advice quickly if needed. It also creates a safe space for experimentation and discovery.

If you're delegating tasks, provide training and then give that person an opportunity to practice that task quickly so you can help guide them and course-correct if needed before they fully take it over and the stakes are higher.

In my role at the healthcare staffing agency, my position evolved dramatically over the years, but none more so than during the pandemic. I was delegating tasks like a maniac because there was just no other choice. To set my team up for success, I had to create opportunities for them to practice the new task they were assigned before the stakes were higher (i.e., when they were presenting to our CEO who has very high expectations). We'd start with a quick kickoff call where I'd explain the task, context, expectations, outcomes, and deadlines and answer any questions. Once they were clear on what was needed, they'd do the task and present it to me in advance of showing it to our CEO. We'd organize full dry runs with them, me, and another team member who was fantastic at giving constructive feedback while still being uplifting. And since the other team member wasn't their boss like I was, their feedback felt more like it came from a friend and cheerleader. The dynamic worked and the person doing the presentation knocked it out of the park almost every time.

It's helpful to allow yourself to participate in these exhibition matches too. As leaders, we are not above the law. We need to practice our skills as well, try new things, and fail fast. When we fail fast, we learn fast. This helps our teams have the psychological safety they need to know it's not only okay to make mistakes, but it is encouraged. Failure is imperative for learning. The quicker you fail, the quicker you innovate and try a new solution.[17] And the only way to let your team fail fast is to release the reins. Micromanagement just won't cut it.

As the ladies at Bossbabe see it, if you don't encourage your employees and support them when they fail, they'll stay in the safe zone trying to avoid failure instead of innovating.[18] This results in them only giving you an idea that they know won't fail. Ultimately, the progress of your business will be slowed, and you'll never even know what amazing ideas you missed out on.

Releasing the reins and delegating is essential to escaping the Type A Trap and avoiding burnout. By failing fast, learning, then iterating and encouraging your team to do the same through exhibition matches, you're helping your team blossom and your organization propel forward. When you personally fail fast as a leader, it also lets your team see transparency from their leadership, which is always a win.

Focus On and Trust People's Strengths

At some point in your career, you may have taken the Strengths-Finder test, which was recently renamed CliftonStrengths.[19] It's one of many similar tests that tells you what your inherent strengths are. But you don't need a test to tell you. Most people already know what comes easily to them, what they enjoy, and what they're just naturally good at. Unfortunately, we're conditioned in life to focus on fixing our weaknesses instead of doubling down on our strengths.

Think about when you were a kid. If you got a report card with a few As, a B, and a D, no doubt, your parents would focus on why you got the D and find a way to help you improve your grade in that subject. It gets conditioned into our heads from a young age that if we can simply improve our weaknesses somehow, we'd be fixed and complete. This can leave us feeling broken and inefficient.[20]

As leaders, focusing on our teams' strengths can be a game-changer in helping them feel empowered, motivated, and, in turn, less burned out. Gallup found that team members feel more confident and productive when they do work that focuses on their strengths instead of their weaknesses. As a result, companies that focus on strength-based leadership see higher employee engagement, increased performance, and lower turnover.[21]

As Elif Suner said in her *Forbes* article on the subject, "The painful part of this approach is that while we have so many valuable resources, we spend a vast amount of our energy trying to get a little bit better on our weaknesses."[22]

Strength-based management is one of the most critical yet often overlooked leadership approaches. Not only does it motivate employees, but it also allows leaders to harness the inherent power and passion of teams to propel organizations forward instead of wallowing in mediocrity by trying to inch someone's weaknesses along. It also allows leaders to release the reins on trying to make every team member good at everything. Instead it helps us focus on what they're inherently good at and find other employees to fill in the gaps.

Trap Talk

"When we're able to put most of our energy into developing our natural talents, extraordinary room for growth exists. So, a revision to the 'you-can-be-anything-you-want-to-be' maxim might be more accurate: 'You cannot be anything you want to be—but you can be a lot more of who you already are.'"—Tom Rath, bestselling author of *StrengthsFinder 2.0*

• • •

Burnout thrives on the overworked and overburdened. When we continue to keep a vice grip on every aspect of our job or life, we create the perfect environment for burnout to fester. Only through releasing the reins, letting go of micromanaging and focusing on empowering others are we able to drive longevity and sustain long-term peak performance.

Release the Reins Jumpstart

- **Do a full life scan.**
  Like a masseuse who scans your body and immediately identifies where you're tight, take the same approach with your life. Do a quick scan: Where are you holding on for dear life? Is it

the one project that gives you direct access to the CEO? Is it the task you feel most competent at? Is it creating a ridiculous approval process so that you feel like you still have your hand in all the things? Put your ego aside and think diligently about what is best for you and your organization or family. This will help you identify areas in which you need to start releasing the reins.

- **Follow these journal prompts.**
  Go buy a cute new journal or dust off the old one you haven't written in for ages. And if all else fails, grab a few sheets of paper or open a new document on your computer. Don't get bogged down in having to have the perfect journal and pen and scenario. Don't overthink it or worry about your penmanship, grammar, or run-on sentences. Just find a quiet place and get writing! Answer these questions:

  - What's the biggest thing you're holding onto right now that you know you need to release?
  - Why are you holding on so tight?
  - What is it that's preventing you from letting go?
  - What are you worried about?
  - What do you fear about releasing the reins?
  - How would you feel if you really let go?
  - What's the first step you need to take to let that shit go?

- **Identify your first exhibition match.**
  Based on your answers from the journal prompt, pick one area to coordinate your first exhibition match. How will you delegate that task? Who will do it? What do they need to know

to be set up for success? Can you get them to do it this week and be there to review their progress? What's the deadline for them taking it over completely?

Keep in mind, these don't have to be epic, grandiose tasks. They could be simple things at work like doing a report or sending meeting recap emails. At home, these could be delegating chores like folding the laundry, picking up the dog poop, or creating a carpool. Again, don't overthink it. Just get started. Like anything, it will get easier the more you do it.

- **Find your hype group.**
  Find or create your hype group for one area of your life. No person or group ticks every box. You'll ultimately need different hype groups for different parts of your life. But start with one today. What area of your life do you feel you need the most support? That's where to focus. Is it your parenting, fitness, relationship, career, faith, finances, or any number of other areas? Start with one and find your group. Begin by looking on Facebook or Meetup for groups with similar interests. Check out your local chamber of commerce, women's groups, faith-based groups, alumni associations for undergrad or grad school, single's groups, parenting groups, etc. Is there someone you follow on social media who you love? They likely have a newsletter list and Facebook group. Join. Reach out to friends who you know are struggling with the same issues, or post something on social media about what you're looking for and create your own group. The possibilities are endless. Once you put it out there that you're looking for a certain group of people, I promise you'll find them, they'll come to you and be just as excited about connecting as you are.

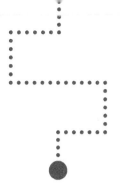

PIVOT LIKE A PRO

Instead of staying the course no matter what and being destination focused, pivot and move with agility.

N o one likes to fail. Especially peak performers. Once we decide we're going to do something, come hell or high water, we stick with it. Sometimes when it feels like things aren't working as they should, instead of sticking our heads up above the water and assessing our path, we dig in deeper. We take the friction as a personal attack. *We will not let it beat us. We will find a way through it.*

I consider this perseverance one of the greatest high-achiever qualities. But sometimes this tenacity blinds us from reality. We continue down roads even after they no longer serve us, simply because we want to accomplish that thing we set out to do.

This can take many forms. Maybe you've stayed too long in a career even though you knew a year in that the industry wasn't for you, but you didn't want to be seen as a quitter. Or you stayed in a relationship you knew wasn't healthy because you didn't want people to judge you for getting divorced. Or maybe you waited too long to let someone go from your team because they were so nice and you felt bad, but instead of sparing them you were just keeping them from thriving in a role that really suited them while slowing overall company growth.

The reality is, we make things harder on ourselves because we're unwilling to question or reassess mid-race. We cage ourselves into processes and circumstances that aren't bringing us closer to our goals—and at times they aren't bringing us *anywhere*. We tread water, wasting our time and valuable potential all because of our pride.

This mindset is a recipe for disaster, a recipe for burnout and falling into the Type A Trap. The good news is there's another way: we must ***pivot like a pro.***

Just as a downhill skier sees a potentially fatal, run-ending patch of ice and pivots left or right on a dime, we need to do the same. Instead of staying the course no matter what and being destination focused, we need to employ a new way of thinking to pivot and move with agility.

Talking Shift

If you're no longer happy in a job, make some adjustments. Or, if it's really bad with no hope of getting better, create an exit strategy, find a new one, and quit. In an unhealthy relationship? Move on. If something is no longer serving you, *pivot.*

This requires a maniacal focus on the alignment between our health and priorities and on how we *actually* end up spending our time, not how we planned to or thought we were spending it. Otherwise, we'll continue to waste time accomplishing things we no longer care about while running ourselves into the ground. This happens when we're not truly paying attention. It happens when we believe we're focusing on growth, but truly we're focusing on others' *perception* of our growth. Pivoting mid-race may confuse those not running with us because they don't see the whole picture. They likely don't know our long-term goals or how they've changed. We often fall into this trap because we're attaching our value and happiness to how others interpret our progress or success instead of what truly brings us joy.

High achievers are elite decision-makers. We take action. It is like a sport for us. This is why it can be incredibly hard for us to understand that our life paths are not black and white. Most people don't just magically wake up one day with a clear picture of what they want in life. (Although we will convince ourselves we *always* know where we want and need to go.) We find out by good old-fashioned trial and error. It's just as important to figure out what we *don't* want to do in life as it is to figure out what we *do* want. And we don't figure any of that out unless we actually take action and DO something!

No amount of reading or researching will compare to actually getting out there, taking action, and pursuing something. And that means we're probably going to try a bunch of things we don't end up liking, then pivoting. And that's okay! Not only is it okay, it's actually how this whole finding yourself and your passions thing works. This is how *life* works. As much as we'd like it to, lightning is not going to strike and make everything crystal clear one day. We've got to get out there, get in the trenches, explore, try, pivot, and try again to find what truly lights us up. We so often rely on our abilities to assess and predict, but really we just need to experience things and allow our feelings and emotions to help lead us to our path.

Type As are such great action takers, just doing, doing, doing all day, but we can also tend to ignore whether the doing is actually moving the needle in the right direction or not. As an old boss of mine used to say, just because we have a tool in our toolkit doesn't mean we have to use it. Sometimes we get so obsessed with taking action and using every arrow in our quiver to try to make progress that we don't realize we're treading water. Yes, pivoting like a pro requires action, but it also requires us to take a realistic assessment of those actions to make sure that they are still moving us in the direction of our desires, hopes, and dreams.

"Business as Usual" Is a Recipe for Failure

It's easy to get on the path to success and stay there. We make some progress, get a few accolades, and just keep plowing ahead. But if we've been following the same road without any significant changes for a period of time, it's important to check on our journey and figure out if we're still inspired, growing, and happy.

When I started my jewelry company, I was so inspired and excited to design, make, market, and sell my pieces. I spent hours coming up with designs, pouring over magazines for inspiration, scouring gem shows for the perfect supplies, taking photos, uploading them to my site, curating the perfect social media posts, creating look books, and more. Everything about the line and its growth excited me. But after a number of years and some success, I found myself dragging my feet to fill orders, less inspired to design, uninterested in sourcing new supplies, and just generally blasé about the whole endeavor. After a few seasons of feeling like I was just going through the motions, I had to ask myself if I really wanted to do it anymore. As much as I loved the brand and enjoyed building it, my interest ultimately shifted. I no longer felt motivated and inspired, and it was time to pivot to the next thing.

When you see your or your business's "usual" way of operating is going to cause you to fall behind in relevance and in competition or in your overall well-being, a swift pivot is necessary. Pivots can be quick, instinctual actions that happen on a moment's notice or small shifts that happen over time with several iterations. Both are beneficial.

Psyched!
Dr. Darria Long

"It's important to think about what is not serving you because it's distracting you from your must-do, most important items. Pivoting isn't about quitting something it's about refocusing your time on those things that are most important."

Sometimes the simplest pivot can prove the most effective. Take PNC Bank for example. One simple change helped them create an army of loyal customers. PNC Bank has a fraction of the branches that some of the larger banks like Wells Fargo and

Bank of America have. In order to increase their market share, they doubled down on their ATMs. With over 60,000 ATMs now nationwide—seven times the size of their branch network—they've been able to grow their customer base outside of where they have branch locations.[1] More importantly, they've made their ATMs act like 24/7 bank tellers so that most customers never even need to go into a branch.

For many families, getting lunch money together for school is part of the weekly routine. As you know, most ATMs only distribute twenty-dollar bills. So, parents often need to go to the ATM and withdraw cash, then make a small purchase somewhere to break the twenties to get the small bills they need for their kids' lunch money. Or parents have to actually go into the bank and stand in line to get what they need. And who has time for that these days?

Understanding that individual and business needs differ greatly, PNC started asking ATM users which type of bills they would like. This simple question now allows anyone using a PNC ATM to withdraw cash in whatever denomination or bills they'd like. Not only does this make getting lunch money easier for your family, but it allows people with lower account balances to take out exactly the amount of cash they need, so they can leave the rest in their account.[2] It's so simple, but it's a game-changer for millions of people. This is a great example of how listening to your customers and pivoting with one small change can save your customers time and create die-hard followers.

Another company that's pivoted to stay relevant and meet their customers where they are is Blue Apron, the leading meal-kit delivery brand. They recently took a cue from restaurants and pivoted their focus to on-demand customers.[3] They started out like all the other meal-kit delivery brands—by sending pre-measured meal kits directly to consumers' homes with all the ingredients for each meal in the box.

But with younger generations being known as on-demand consumers, Blue Apron knew they were missing an important piece of the market. So instead of making consumers sign up for costly weekly subscriptions, Blue Apron took a chance, pivoted, and got creative to stay ahead of their competition. They started selling weekly meal boxes at Costco, offering on-demand single meals on delivery platforms like GrubHub and Postmates, and broadened their meal choices to accommodate a wider spectrum of consumers who wanted things like gluten- and dairy-free options. These proactive pivots helped Blue Apron change with the evolving tastes of their target market and separate themselves from the ever-growing competitor meal-kit brands while helping them increase revenue.

One last example of a company pivoting and moving with agility makes my eighties baby heart sing. If you were a kid in the eighties, you know that Nintendo was life. The popular gaming company is the perfect example of how small, intentional pivots over time can lead to long-term success.

Most know Nintendo from their incredibly popular Nintendo Entertainment System (NES) that launched in 1985. I can't tell you how many hours my brother and I spent playing their iconic games such as *Super Mario Bros.*, *The Legend of Zelda*, *Duck Hunt,* and *Donkey Kong* or blowing into the game cartridges to clear out the dust to make them work again in the system. (If you know, you know.) But the company actually started back in 1889 as a playing card company.[4] Who knew?

In 1949, after the founder had a stroke, his twenty-two-year-old grandson took over the company and spent the next sixty-three years pivoting like a pro until he found his gaming groove. Over the years, Nintendo offered several diverse products and services such as taxis, instant rice, hourly hotels, and toys. It wasn't until they created the arcade version of *Donkey Kong* in 1980 that they really hit their stride. The game and its main character paved the way for the NES release in 1985 and *Super Mario Bros.*, which was the best-selling gaming franchise for three decades. And Nintendo is still going strong. Their latest system, the Nintendo Switch, was the best-selling console in 2021 in the United States, Europe, and Japan, and continues to cement Nintendo as one of the most successful gaming companies in the world.[5]

My dad, who is a creature of habit, as most of us are, always jokes that he likes to get in a good rut and stay there. But this mindset is a recipe for disaster, falling into the Type A Trap, and burning out. Smart companies and people pivot like pros.

Personal Pivots Are Priceless

The world moves quickly. Not only do we need to move and adapt to changing times, we need to move with agility to our changing hopes, dreams, goals, passions, and desires. It's natural to change. It's normal to evolve. It's part of growing and maturing. Just because you said you were going to do something doesn't mean you have to stay with it if you decide you don't like it or it's not working.

As Type A high achievers, when we set a path for ourselves, we have a compulsive desire to see it through, but sometimes that isn't the best way. When we notice we're unfulfilled or unhappy along the way, we need to give ourselves permission to pivot into a new direction that will bring us happiness and alignment. This is most clearly demonstrated in our careers but applies to our personal lives as well.

Nothing makes this clearer than what we've seen during the Great Resignation. People, especially Americans, have been living to work for a long time.[6] All of a sudden, they're saying, "You know what? Screw this. I'm outta here. This isn't what I want to do with my life. Life is short, and this just isn't worth it." Millions of people have left their jobs and continue to leave. They're finally asking themselves the important questions they've likely ignored for perhaps their entire career until now. Questions like: *What do I want to do with my life? When do I feel happiest and most alive?* And *If not now, when?*

People are beginning to make career decisions not just based off financial gain or convenience, but because they're realizing they aren't aligned with what lights them up. A new report from the global education tech firm Cengage Group found that while burnout ranked high, other factors such as reconsidering their priorities and professional goals, not feeling aligned with the work, and having desires to pursue other passions and career paths were huge factors in why people are quitting their jobs.[7]

The pandemic has forced a major shift in consciousness in the workforce, especially with younger professionals. While critics may argue that many originally quit their jobs and didn't return to the workforce to sit at home and collect unemployment benefits, the truth is that people have reevaluated their lives, pivoted, and found new careers and opportunities that align better with their goals, desires, and lifestyles.[8]

If you're lucky, you know from day one what you want to do with your life. My mom is this person. She always knew she wanted to work in theater. She got a bachelor's and a master's degree in theater, was a performer, a theatrical makeup artist, an acting teacher, and then spent twenty-five years as an executive director at one of the country's most elite performing arts schools. Her entire career was in theater, and she could not have been any happier.

Alas, that's not how it always goes. In fact, that's rarely how it goes. I can't tell you how many times I've seen family members and friends get paralyzed trying to figure out what they want to do with their lives. They think if they research long enough, eventually they're going to figure out what their passion is and what they should do with their lives. But they don't actually take action, put themselves out there, and try something. It's frustrating to watch. People are so afraid to jump in and feel their way through experiences to find out what lights them up. We can't possibly know for sure until we try, and there is inherent risk in that—sometimes we hit the jackpot quickly and other times we swim around in discomfort for a while before we hit gold.

Here's the thing: We often don't realize we're in a rut. We run around on a well-worn path and don't even realize how long we're slogging through the same circles. It can be obvious to others that we need to pivot and take action, but we don't see it. Ultimately, that's how we learn what we do and don't like, what works and what doesn't.

Trap Talk

As MTV star, author, and keynote speaker Ben Nemtin says, "Sometimes you get so caught up on the treadmill that you forget to check in and see what you really want. It's not that you're not listening to your voice, you don't know how to. You're not able to listen to it, and you don't even know what

> that voice is. You wonder if it's your voice, what you think
> you need to do for your ego or validation, what you think
> you're supposed to do, or what you thought you wanted."

I've personally pivoted careers at least six times. And my life of trial and error even started in college. I started out as a French major, then changed to communications, and then to political science. When I started my career and got my first real job, I was a low-level advertising assistant at a small digital agency in London. This was back in the day when NO ONE was interested in digital advertising. We were the dark and dirty people pounding the pavement selling banners, skyscrapers, and pop ups, but it was a fun time to be in a budding industry.

I worked my way up and then was poached by MTV Networks Europe, where I became the head of digital advertising. We then had a death in our family, and I moved back to Los Angeles. This felt like a good time to do something different. I had long been interested in fashion, but my parents always wanted me to get a "real" job, so advertising it was. It was a super creative industry and the closest thing to fashion that still allowed for a steady job that paid the bills.

But after doing advertising for a few years, it was time to pivot. The unexpected death in our family and abrupt move back to Southern California felt like the right time to follow my initial dreams of working in fashion. It's amazing how death and grief can often bring about change and realign us with our passions and desires.

I didn't want to be a fashion designer though. That wasn't my thing. I was really good at putting outfits together and picking out clothes for people that worked for their body type, style, and lifestyle . . . so into the world of styling it was. I started where anyone starts: I looked for work on Craigslist. Or at least that was where any normal person looking to break into a new industry started fifteen years ago. And sure enough, after a quick search I found a listing for an assistant to a celebrity stylist.

Let me preface this by saying that everyone in Los Angeles calls themselves a "celebrity something"—celebrity chef, trainer, hairstylist, manicurist, dry cleaner, whatever. Usually that means they've tenuously worked with someone who was an extra in some D-list movie. But a celebrity? Not quite.

To my surprise, after getting the gig, it was indeed legit. Day one I was at Jessica Simpson's house in Beverly Hills (back when she was in her prime) dressing her for some awards show. What quickly followed can only be described as an absolute crash course in the Hollywood fashion machine. I dressed everyone from Heather Locklear, Christie Brinkley, and Christina Applegate to Diane Lane, Ellen Pompeo, Allison Janney, and Jenna Dewan for the Academy Awards, Emmy Awards, Golden Globe Awards, movie premieres, editorial shoots, TV appearances, and more. *It was insane!*

One minute I'm sitting in my childhood bedroom at my parents' house depressed about the state of my life and the next minute I'm dressing celebs backstage at the MTV Movie & TV Awards, chit chatting with Britney, Rihanna, and Beyoncé. It was a true pinch-me moment. But like most things, it sounds better than it actually was.

After enough emotional abuse from working for someone who is a real-life *The Devil Wears Prada*, I knew it was time to take what I'd learned and pivot! I started working with my own clients, non-celebrities, or "normal people" as I called them, and then ventured into fashion journalism. I started writing for a few different magazines and websites and styled countless editorial spreads. I developed relationships with every major boutique owner in Southern California because I was pulling clothes from them for photo shoots and writing profile pieces about them for various magazines.

It wasn't long before I pivoted again into traditional journalism. I had always wanted to work in news and figured now that I was technically a fashion journalist, I could parlay that into "real" news. I started as an assignment editor and then moved into digital editor and field producer for a local station in Sacramento. But after a couple years of terrible pay, even worse hours, and work that didn't excite me, it was time to pivot again.

That career led me to working on the creative team of a full-service advertising and marketing agency. While at that job, I started my jewelry business on the side and ultimately ended up being in about fifty stores all over the county—because all those boutique owners I had established relationships with as a stylist were happy to put my jewelry in their stores.

One thing that's important to remember is that when we pivot, all that we've already built, accomplished, and experienced is not lost. Even if your pivot seems like it's taking you on a completely unrelated path, those experiences can come full circle and show you meaning you couldn't see before. Not only meaning, but they can set you up for unexpected success in your next iteration.

Psyched!
Dr. Madelyn Blair

"Pivoting has to do with confidence in yourself. If you know who you are (values, skills, talents) and what your purpose is, the pivoting act is grounded, you know it, and the pivot will not uproot you. When you know these things and you see that your life is filling up with what works against your purpose and values, it's time to look for another option. The secret is taking the time to know your purpose and your values. When you do, and you are confident that these are really true for you, then every act you do is piece by piece making your life one that works toward your purpose and is consistent with your values. You can always look yourself in the mirror. Also, the pivot doesn't have to be life changing. It may be small, consistent changes over time."

After being away from home for nearly a decade and maxing out in pay at the mom-and-pop agency I was working at, I decided I was ready to move back to Southern California to be closer to my family and work for a kick-ass organization with tons of room for growth. I knew I wanted to live in San Diego and that I wanted to work for an incredible company with smart people, a great company culture, plenty of money for raises, amazing benefits, and all that jazz.

I could write another book on how to get a killer job, but in short, I googled "best companies to work for in San Diego" and then focused my search on those companies. After a few months of proactive searching and interviews, I landed my job as the head of marketing for the largest healthcare staffing company in the country. Then, after six years there and a global pandemic, I parlayed that knowledge into a speaking career.

All that to say, I've pivoted careers *many* times. Every time, I take what I've learned and repackage it to support my next vision for my life. Each stop isn't a waste of time, but rather an additional layer that gets added to the richness of my life and résumé. I believe each step makes me an even more interesting person and an even better candidate for my next job. Pivoting and moving with agility is what propels you forward in life and your career. It should be seen as a positive, enriching part of life, not as failure.

Get Shifting Now

Pay Attention to Your Jokes

Pay attention to what you're "joking" about. We all make jokes throughout the day. Sometimes they're self-deprecating, sometimes they're at other people's expense, and most times they tell us everything we need to know about what's going on in our lives.

If there is a particular person or circumstance that's always the butt of your jokes, take it as a sign that it's time to pivot. I know when I was deep in the throes of my burnout, I was constantly making jokes at my job's expense. There wasn't a day that went by that I wasn't saying something disparaging about them. These can be very subtle as well. You know the drill—someone asks you how work is going, and you say with sarcasm, "Oh, you know, just living the dream," implying that it's a nightmare and not how you want to spend your time.

I hear similar jokes constantly from girlfriends who aren't happy with their weight. I ask if they want to have a pool or beach day and before the words even get out of my mouth they're making some disparaging, half-joking-but-totally-serious remark about their body in a bathing suit. Even just these small, seemingly insignificant jokes and remarks are a tell-tale sign that there is a much larger problem brewing under the surface waiting to explode at any moment.

Trap Talk

Danielle Noble, a partner at a leading law firm, says, "Listen to what you're saying to yourself. Are you beating yourself up the whole time? How long does that negative self-talk go on for? We all have negative self-talk, but how long does it last? If it's a few minutes or maybe an hour, fine. But if it's lasting all day, week, or even longer, we've got a real problem."

Sure, we can all make jokes about things and people we love, but when those jokes continue for days, weeks, months, or even years, it's imperative that we pivot. We owe it to ourselves to recognize the signs of a problem and address it head on instead of continuing to suffer through something that no longer serves us.

Who Do You Envy?

Envy is a funny thing. On the one hand, it can be incredibly motivating and inspire you to take action to create the life you desire. But on the other hand, it can tell you a lot about the current state of your life and changes that you need to make.

Envy shows up in many places. I notice it most when I'm scrolling social media. That might be where you find it often as well. I follow some incredible people on social media, and, even though I know it's just a highlight reel of their lives, I get envious of the lives they live.

There's a well-known keynote speaker I follow who I find myself envying constantly. He lives such an interesting life. He lives at the beach, exercises daily, is always outside doing something fun, travels a ton for work and even more for play, creates fun experiences for himself and his friends, and just generally seems to really enjoy life. I get so envious of his life. I look at him and think, *That's what I want to do! How do I make that my life?*

The good news is that instead of letting that envy fester and turn into something negative, I've been able to take his life as inspiration for what is possible and start making changes in my life that can help me get closer to leading my version of that life.

If you're wondering whether it's time for a pivot or not, think about if you're envying a certain person or situation frequently? One of the *New York Times*–bestselling authors I interviewed found herself envying her single friends all the time. She envied their girl trips, happy hours, bougie dinners, and general lack of stress from their husbands. After noticing how much envy was seeping into her thoughts and feelings, she took a critical look at her life. She realized her marriage was not healthy and that a change was needed. This is the same woman who also used to check her phone religiously, praying for a family emergency so she could stop working. She was obviously burned out in more than one area of her life.

It's normal to envy certain people and situations from time to time. But when that envy starts consuming your life and being something that happens daily or every time you log into social media, take that as a glaring red flag that it's time for a pivot in your life. So ask yourself: Who or what do you envy? The answer to this question will help you determine whether it's time to make a change both personally and professionally.

Check Your Passion/Proficiency Meter

Pivots come in all shapes and sizes. We often think of a pivot as leaving one thing behind for another. But the truth is, pivots can take the form of doubling down on learning, education, and deepening your proficiency on a particular topic.

Trap Talk

If you're wondering whether it's time to pivot or not, use this tip from registered nurse and healthcare workforce expert April Hansen: "Check your passion/proficiency meter," she says. "Have you lost your passion? Or are you just not proficient enough at something?" If you're simply not proficient, that's a pretty easy fix. If you've lost your passion, then it's time to pivot.

The passion/proficiency meter April mentions is so simple, but it works every time. We often feel burned out when we've lost our passion for something. For me, those are the easiest pivots to recognize. You were once excited about something, and now you're not. It's clear that you've lost your passion, and it's time for a pivot. But your passion may just need a little fuel added to fire it up again. For example, if you're an artist and you've lost your passion, get yourself to a museum stat. Immerse yourself in great art, take a class, attend a lecture, watch YouTube videos, and you just might find your passion again. If that still doesn't help, then yes, perhaps it's time for a pivot.

Alternatively, sometimes we're just not proficient enough at our job or hobby and that is leading us to burnout. In that case, a little education and help is what's needed. This could be a class at your local junior college, attending a lecture or webinar by an expert in the field, watching YouTube videos, or taking an online course by someone halfway around the world. The beauty of the Internet and the world today is that we can study with experts anywhere in the world and usually, if done virtually, for a fraction of the price.

So next time you're feeling burned out, ask yourself this: *Have I lost my passion? Or do I just need a bit more help so I can feel more proficient at this task?* The answer to these questions will help you determine whether it's time to pivot like a pro or not.

Make Time for Your Passion Projects

When we're burned out, finding time to do one more thing sounds like death. I get it. I felt the same way. But making even the smallest changes in one area of your life will give you space to make a bigger pivot later. Pivots can be cumulative, and several small changes eventually add up to one large pivot.

We all have hopes, dreams, goals, aspirations, passions, and things we want to do, see, and accomplish in our lives. Unfortunately, life happens, and these things often go by the wayside—especially when we're burned out. We make time for everyone else's things, but not our own.

Have you ever noticed how we have deadlines for everything

in life except for our own goals? We say to ourselves, *I'll work on it tomorrow. I'll find time next week. Maybe next year I'll do it.* There will always be someone else's priority to put first. Always. But if we don't make time for our own goals, we'll never achieve them. This can lead us to feel even more burned out because we don't have time to do the things we really want to do. That's why it's important to carve out time for our goals. Even if it's just ten minutes a day to start.

In the depths of my burnout, I was doing nothing but rolling out of bed, making coffee, and sitting at my desk in my pajamas until at least 2:00 p.m. when I'd feel too gross to carry on. I'd then take a quick shower and sit back at my desk until well after dark, often until 10:00 p.m., then roll into bed and do it all over again the next day.

I was miserable. Miserable! That wasn't a life. It was the definition of a rat race and not a race I wanted to be in. I knew I wanted out and had to find a better way. But unlike the millions who quit their jobs during the Great Resignation, I wasn't able to. Or perhaps more accurately, *I chose not to.*

I was making great money, needed the money, and didn't want to just quit and have no income. That's not how I like to roll. I'm such an independent woman that I always like to be able to support myself. I've watched too many girlfriends get stuck in unhealthy relationships with schmucks they can't stand simply because they can't afford to leave. I don't ever want that to be me. I love knowing that at any moment I could say, "You know what? Screw this. I'm out of here." And just leave. That's also probably why I stayed single for so long and didn't get married until I was forty-one, but I digress.

During my burnout I knew I had to find a way out of my day

job. It was slowly killing me and robbing me of any joy I once had. I needed a way out. I had always thought about being a keynote speaker and was inspired by so many I knew and the lives they lived; I figured now was as good a time as any to start pursuing that dream. It was something I'd done on the side on various topics over the years, but I never took it seriously enough to make it a full-time gig. But when I burned out, I needed something fun, something that fed my soul, something that made me feel like I had an exit strategy from my day job.

So, I signed up for a virtual keynote speaker bootcamp that was happening a few weeks later and that was it. I took the boot camp, then signed up for private coaching, attended an in-person boot camp, and met the most amazing people who were smart, accomplished, and successful and who were leading the most interesting lives. I felt like I had met my people, and all I wanted to do was spend more time with them and speak on more stages.

By investing in courses and coaches (thanks to the income I still had from my day job), I was able to get the fast pass to getting my keynote speaking career up and running. Yes, it was more work that I was adding to my already-busy day, but it was *my* work on *my* terms for *my* future. It literally gave me life during a low time because I could finally see my exit strategy from my day job. All I needed to do was carve out a little time each day, do the things my coaches told me to do, and put in the hard yards.

And the funny thing is, by investing in myself and my passion, I found increased passion for my day job again. I started coming up with new ideas and initiatives for my department. I reengaged with my team and colleagues. By taking time to focus on myself and my passions outside of work, I also reignited my passions at work. It was a win-win.

Trap Talk

Lisi Harrison, one of the *New York Times* bestselling authors I interviewed, shared her thoughts on this exact subject. She says, "Things that happen in our life that seem like tragedies and major disrupters are actually good. They move us to a new place and eradicate the burnout."

I could not agree more. Burnout felt debilitating to me. It turned my life upside down and completely knocked the wind out of me. But it led me to follow a passion that I had buried for years, which in turn breathed new life into every area of my life, including my day job that was the major contributor to my burnout in the first place.

Reengage at Work

If you're anything like me and you didn't feel like it was possible to just quit your job to join the Great Resignation and follow your dreams, but you've fallen out of love with your job and have quietly quit, this one's for you. Sometimes we just fall into a rut and need a few tips for reengaging with our jobs. If that's the case, try these:

Stand up and get noticed.[9]
Tell your boss what you've been up to, your projects, accomplishments, and ideas for new initiatives. Be visible. I felt like I was disappearing by the day, so I started an internal TV show for our corporate employees. I hosted the show and produced it with a small team. It helped me be visible again in the company, and, most importantly, it filled a hole in their corporate communications that was desperately needed.

Go into the office a couple days a week.

Yes, most of us prefer working from home, but merely existing in your tiny house can be a recipe for insanity. Heading into the office a couple days a week can give you a change of scenery, help you cross paths with colleagues you haven't seen in a while, and remind you why you used to like your job.

Reimagine your job.

If you feel like you're lacking purpose in your job, reconfigure it! Managers don't want to lose good employees like you. So take this as an opportunity to redefine your role. We talk about this in Mindset Shift #1: *decode your flow.* This is the time to get rid of tasks that don't serve you—volunteer to start a new project or initiative that aligns with your passions.

Reframe your thinking.

Instead of dwelling on all the annoying small tasks you have to do, focus on the bigger picture. How does what you do in your role help the company reach its goals? How is your company affecting change in the world? You're a part of that.

Build your personal brand.

If you want to move up in the company, dress the part. When you log into a Zoom call, make sure you look presentable. Better yet, make sure you look better and more professional than everyone else on the call. Buy a small, inexpensive light off Amazon to ensure you've got good lighting, clear out the clutter behind you so everything in frame looks polished, throw on a blazer, do your hair and makeup. Make an effort; it will not go unnoticed.

Take your personal brand one step further by building out your LinkedIn profile.
Write thought leadership articles, comment on posts and conversations you want to be a part of, tag your favorite thought leaders, engage with them in their comments, share your knowledge and passion. Attend local networking events and post about them online. Reach out to people who are in similar roles or roles you'd like to be in and ask them a question. Start cultivating a relationship. People naturally want to help. When you up your game with your personal brand, everyone at your company will start to see you as "that person" in the best possible way. They'll know that you are the one to go to for answers and that you're a thought leader on your subject.

There are countless ways you can step up to reengage at work. Put your own spin on these to fall back in love with your day job—or at least make it tolerable until you can find your next gig or build your business enough to pursue it full time.

• • •

I know these pivots can be scary. No one likes change. It's difficult, uncomfortable, and often affects a lot more people than just us. It can often have adverse effects in the short term but is always completely worth it in the long term.

So instead of staying destination focused because we said we were going to do something, we have to move with agility and pivot like a pro to make sure the way we spend our time today continues to align with our hopes, dreams, and passions. Because ultimately, you're only letting yourself down and feeding burnout by holding onto something that no longer serves you.

Pivot Like a Pro Jumpstart

- **Log it.**

  Create a new note on your phone and start keeping track of what you're making jokes about and who or what situations you're envying. Sometimes these are so quick to come out of our mouths (or pop up into our minds) that we don't even realize we're doing them. Now is the time to take note of what you're saying and log it. At the end of the week, review your notes and see what sticks out. You can also ask your partner or anyone you spend a lot of time with to help you with this as well. I bet they could tell you immediately what you always make jokes about. Let them help you with this process.

- **Take a class.**

  If you're feeling burned out, and you've realized it's because you aren't proficient enough at what you're trying to accomplish, it's time to get help. Enroll in a class at your local junior college, register for an online course, watch free YouTube videos, or binge-watch TED Talks. Whatever form it takes, register for a class today or schedule study time on your calendar this week.

- **Find fifteen minutes.**

  Finding time to pursue our passions is often the hardest time to find. Kids need a ride somewhere? We find the time. Boss needs something done tomorrow? We find the time. Partner has a crisis we need to deal with? We find the time. Yet finding time for our own goals feels damn near impossible. But not this week. Get up fifteen minutes earlier tomorrow. Use those fifteen extra minutes to pursue your goal. It could be as simple as sending someone an email for help, doing research on what the first steps are to becoming x, writing a page, or hell, even a paragraph of your first blog post or creating a social media post. Whatever it is, just start. Dial that alarm back fifteen minutes and start tomorrow. I don't care if it's at 4:00 a.m. You'll feel more fulfilled all day knowing you've made one small step in the direction of your dreams. Then keep it up!

- **Build your profile.**
  What do you want to be known for? How do you want people to think about you? It's time to build out your profile. If you're single, build out that online dating profile. If you're looking to pivot careers, build out your LinkedIn profile. Wherever you're ready to pivot, it's time to make it social media official. Putting it out there in writing is scientifically proven to make it more likely to happen. So own it and put it out into the universe today.

- **Follow journal prompts.**
  As my late friend Brenda Kinsell used to ask in her personal style classes: What are you moving away from and what are you moving toward? Pivots can be complex, multifaceted puzzles that affect your whole family. To help bring you clarity on your pivot, ask yourself what you are moving away from. After you get that out, ask yourself what you are moving toward. The answers to these questions will help you notice the small nuances of your pivots and help shed light on all the areas that may be affected by each pivot.

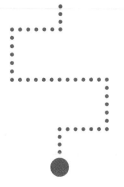

SLOW DOWN TO SPEED UP

Instead of maxing out each race, shift to methodical marathon
planning with a focus on durability and self-care.

Slowing down doesn't come easy for many, certainly not me. That's something *those* people do, not us over-eager over-achievers. I get FOMO when I slow down. But it's not fear of missing out on a brunch or an outing with friends, it's fear that it's going to take me even longer to accomplish my goals. I feel guilty and lazy watching TV instead of reading yet another leadership or personal development book to further my career. I tell myself I can't relax until I clear out my inbox, return that call, finish that project, the laundry is done, the car is washed, sheets are changed, toys are picked up, dog is walked, I've worked out, showered, gone to the grocery store, started dinner, etc., etc., etc.

The list is literally never ending. When I'm resting, I think about everything I should be doing and how if I put off that thing one more day, my goal is going to take even longer to achieve or I'm going to miss out on an opportunity. But when I'm executing the to-do list, I feel like I should be taking care of myself and relaxing. It's a constant battle of always thinking I should be doing something else. I know I need to be present where I am and take the time I need to rest, reset, and recharge. I even get annoyed with my husband when he spends the whole weekend sleeping in and watching Netflix instead of actually doing something I consider productive. It's been beaten into my head that my productivity determines my worth, so slowing down actually causes me anxiety instead of helping me de-stress.

When I untangled this concept a bit more, it led me to discovering mindset shift #4: ***slow down to speed up.*** I realized that when I'm in constant go, go, go mode, my mind is not focused or thinking strategically. It's simply trying to cross as many things as possible off my never-ending to-do list. But on those rare occasions that I allow myself to just stop, breathe, and enjoy a moment of silence or stillness, I have a breakthrough on a project or situation that I've been stuck on.

I remember feeling completely flustered and overwhelmed about finishing the first draft of this book. I wanted it done so badly, so I could get it into people's hands and also continue to grow my speaking career. One day I was driving in my car on my way to Pilates. I was running a tad late and felt that uneasy feeling of driving a little too fast, a little too close to the car in front of me, getting annoyed when people took too long to turn, and running every yellow light to make sure I got to class on time. I had music blaring in my car and at one point it all got to be too much, someone cut in front of me, and I felt like I was going to cry. I turned the music off and drove the rest of the way in silence.

My mind was overloaded; my senses were overloaded; my *plate* was overloaded. By the time I arrived at Pilates ten minutes of silence later, I felt better. It took finding a moment of silence to realize that 1) who cares if I'm a couple minutes late to Pilates? It doesn't matter. And 2) I had put a ridiculous amount of pressure on myself to reach an arbitrary deadline. Literally nothing was going to happen if I didn't make this first draft deadline that I had placed on myself. Would I be a failure if the book came out a week or two later? No! Who cares?

So instead of sprinting and maxing out each race like we usually do, being proud of the ridiculous schedules we keep and falling into the Type A Trap, we need to shift our thinking to methodical marathon planning and a focus on durability and self-care.

Talking Shift

Like many of the peak performers I interviewed, we don't know how to slow ourselves down. When we go after anything, we go at it like a freight train. When chatting with the Guinness World Records holder for World's Fittest Man, he told me that when he decides he's going to do something, he can't let it go. He constantly psychoanalyzes himself, wondering if there is anything he can do better. Once he set his sights on the world record, he knew he would get it or die trying.

As Type As, we're always in a hurry. We walk fast wherever we go, we drive fast, tailgate people, and are quick to give people a courtesy honk if they don't accelerate the second the light turns green. We type a million words per minute, cram as many things as we can into each day, and even when we're supposedly relaxing, we over plan, filling our day with yoga, massages, meditation, reading, you name it. We shove it all into our one "relaxing" day because we just can't help ourselves. If we're going to take time away from accomplishing our goals to relax, then we need to know that we're doing it well and making the most of our time relaxing. We always have to feel like we're accomplishing something, even if that something is relaxing—the very antithesis of what we think of as "accomplishing."

But this constant fixation on doing, accomplishing, and going keeps our body and brain in a state of turmoil and unrest. We also often only relax or "decompress" when we've hit a point where we can't ignore the buildup in our minds and bodies any longer—which is usually when our physical and mental symptoms make it impossible for us to keep the pace we've been running at. So, we stop for a few seconds, take a couple bubble baths and cancel a meeting or two, and we think we're all patched up and ready to roll again.

We run on pure adrenaline and excitement, and that does not give us time to actually think, process, and plan to the best of our abilities. As much as we don't want to hear it, slowing down will actually help us to speed up in the long term. Just like in business, we may need to make a short-term sacrifice for long-term success, same goes with our need to slow down. We may hate it at the time, but allowing our body to decompress and our mind to have time to truly rest and just be will give us space for breakthroughs, progress, and forward motion in the future.

While counterintuitive, slowing down will actually help us achieve our goals faster and provide more accurate precision in our goal setting because we are coming at it from a state of rest and clarity as opposed to hustle, grind, and grit. But we need to incorporate stillness and rest into our *regular* routines, not just when we're having a mental breakdown.

Vacations Won't Fix Everything, but They're a Good Start

As Type A overachievers, we rarely allow ourselves to fully detach from our daily grind. Even when we "take a break," we find sneaky ways to stay connected to our goals and ambitions. The thought of actually unplugging and taking time away results in fear that we're going to let all our progress slip away. However, the exact opposite happens—we're not able to perform at our highest levels because we never let ourselves rest and refuel.

Have you ever gone on vacation only to spend the whole time working on your side hustle because you finally have time away from your day job? Do you look forward to a weekend with no plans so you can finally get to ALL the things on your to-do list instead of spending time relaxing? Or worse yet, have you taken a sick day because you are legitimately sick, but feel like you should be tackling some item on your list instead of actually resting and regrouping? I'm right there with you.

When we never stop to rest and recharge, we're in a constant fight-or-flight state. We can see the effects of burnout materialize in so many areas of our lives, and they come on much faster when we force ourselves to keep moving and keep working, no matter how we feel. Do you pull clumps of hair out of your shower drain every day? You've probably got too much stress in your life. Are you struggling to get a full night's sleep without taking a cocktail of sleep aides, yet you still wake up exhausted? That's burnout talking. Are you constantly anxious, going through a million what-if scenarios in your head, dwelling in the past or panicking about things that haven't even happened and may never? You're on the burnout fast track.[1]

Psyched!
Dr. Marsha Chinichian

"I have had many C-suite clients who have brought up sleep issues in sessions. A common pattern was their intense schedules that are nonstop with back-to-back meetings and stress. When this happens, our minds are overly occupied all day long with work and then after work with family/ kids. There isn't time to just relax the mind and allow thoughts to show up on their own, which leads to creativity and improved problem-solving skills. This can lead to disrupted sleep by being woken up at night with thoughts of work or other topics. One recommendation is making room and space for these thoughts by writing them down or just sitting in silence without an agenda for a period of time each day. If you don't make the space your thoughts will show up unannounced at their will, not yours."

It's hard for us to admit that our constant need for productivity isn't always physical. Yes, we stay up late to get those reports done. We show up to the office even though we know we should go to the doctor. And we never let our endless list of errands get the best of us. However, a major aspect of this struggle is unseen. In the moments when we're meant to rest and recharge, we lack the ability to honor our mental boundaries too. We tell ourselves we will unplug, but we still let stresses and thoughts from work and everyday life take over our minds, preventing us from being present, which is what refills our tank so we can show up post-break.

Statistics show that Americans are overworked and rarely take all their vacation time. In 2023, Americans failed to cash in more than 765 million vacation days.[2] Regardless of how much you love your job, consciously scheduling time with your family for your health and traveling not only benefits you, but the practice strengthens your company as well.

The CEO of Acceleration Partners is so serious about unplugging that he pays his employees $750 to stay offline during vacation.[3] That sounds good, right? His reasoning? Recharging and self-care are part of high performance. Even the world's greatest athletes understand the value of interval training, and they make rest a part of the training process. But many employees don't realize the clear link between vacations and performance.

Harvard Business Review even found that employees who took more than eleven vacation days per year had a 30 percent higher chance of earning a raise or promotion. High performers take more vacation time, get their work done in less time, and know that taking time to recharge is vital to their durability and role as an A-player.

But many people fear taking time off because they don't want to overburden their team, or they think the company can't function without them. But the truth is, people who refuse to take time off aren't saving their colleagues, they are often just avoiding delegation.

However, simply promoting self-care and offering paid vacations isn't enough. The onus is on leaders, on us, to create a culture where vacation is part of the work cycle and employees are empowered and expected to take time off. By tying in a financial incentive, Acceleration Partners showed their team that they consider vacations a positive benefit for everyone involved. They want their employees to be happy and engaged, but they also believe vacation time improves the health and durability of the business.

Betabrand, the e-commerce apparel company known for their crowdsourced products, took a slightly different approach to help their employees slow down to speed up. After the CEO learned that many of his employees hadn't traveled outside the country, he got creative to get them to take time off and travel without worrying about how they were going to pay for it.[4]

He consolidated the company's spending onto one corporate credit card that earned frequent flyer miles for every purchase. He saved them up and now sends staffers on their dream trips at no extra cost to them. Betabrand covers the flight and four nights in a hotel. All employees have to do is submit a place they've always wanted to visit and why and a winner is picked every four to six weeks.

Spending money is also covered through "fun raisers," where a hat is passed during happy hours to gather donations for the lucky traveler. That way, everyone is personally invested in the traveler's experience. The CEO is so passionate about international travel and taking this time off that employees' personal vacation time isn't docked for these trips either.

This type of all-hands-supported travel has had a huge impact on encouraging a positive company culture. While it costs the company nothing financially, it's been a game-changer in creating a team-oriented culture, broadening employees' experiences and mindsets, and preventing burnout and turnover.

Both Acceleration Partners and Betabrand illustrate the importance of leadership mentoring and coaching employees on the importance of self-care. If we, as leaders, aren't preaching these concepts to our teams, aren't following these practices ourselves, and aren't taking care of our own physical and mental health, then why would we think our employees would? It's up to us to set a good example for our employees to focus on their physical and mental health to not only prevent burnout but to help them be healthier and happier in all areas of their lives.

The same is true whether you work in the corporate world or not. If you, as a parent, friend, caretaker, etc., are not taking time for yourself, then you won't be able to care for others at the highest level and won't give other people permission to take care of themselves. Parents especially need to model this practice for their kids. Observing this behavior will teach children that honoring themselves and their wellness is their first priority.

Chris Runkle, the former diplomat and presidential aide I interviewed says, "You need to sit back and think in a long-term sense. Most people don't do this. They think life is transactional. It's not. It's on a long curve, and you have to pick your opportunities and meet your requirements as you go along that road."

Runkle's comments illustrate that dealing with this issue of burnout isn't a switch that is flipped. Instead, it's like slowly turning around a cruise ship—it takes time and intention. Our behaviors now will set the stage for us well into the future.

Psyched!
Dr. Madelyn Blair

"Slowing down requires that you stay in touch with your purpose as you make your moment-to-moment decisions. I recommend to my own clients that they choose only three things to do during the day and then do them. This feels impossible until you try it. Suddenly, attempting to restrict your list to three, the items reflect awareness of the larger picture even as you are doing them. It keeps your eye on the bigger, long-term purpose effortlessly."

Joe Decker, the Guinness World Records holder for World's Fittest Man, echoes Runkle's thoughts. He says, "I almost died after the world record. I was in bad shape. I almost worked out so much that I killed myself. I had the immune system of an HIV patient and had a mental breakdown. Until we find that balance, it's hard. Balance isn't something we're good at. It's something we have to work on."

Yes, vacations are great. But if we aren't making fundamental changes in our daily routines, mindsets, and habits, we will simply fall right back into our old habits that lead to burnout when we get back. We see this with the Great Resignation. People are frustrated and burned out at work, they quit, only to take another job and feel burned out again because they haven't changed any of their behaviors that led to their burnout at their last job. It's a vicious cycle. But by learning how to slow down in large and small ways in your daily life, you can help prevent the ongoing cycle of burnout.

We Can't Work Our Way Out of Burnout

Most Type A high achievers are self-aware enough to catch onto the fact that we do, in fact, need to practice rest and self-care to stay healthy and able to chase our dreams and accomplish our goals. However, if we're not careful, we'll turn this easeful, intuitive practice into another intense to-do list. When we turn slowing down into another high-impact, over-scheduled goal, we're missing the point of turning away from the grind to serve our mind and soul.

When I burned out, I looked at recovering from burnout as the next thing I was going to "accomplish." If I was going to come back from it, there would be no one that recovered from burnout better than me. The true definition of a Type A personality—even in my defeat I felt like I needed to be the best.

So off I went, picking up every possible burnout recovery and self-care tool I could think of. If I read an article and it mentioned some skills, supplement, or technique, I added that to the list. I learned how to do transcendental meditation and meditated twice a day, got acupuncture twice a week, nutritional IVs twice a week, went to therapy, got massages and facials, took ALL the vitamins, changed my diet, tried a morning gratitude practice, saw every doctor, and more. My schedule was so jam-packed with every recovery tool I could think of. I was like, *Am I relaxed yet?!* Needless to say, I wasn't.

I had itemized self-care to the point of stress. If you looked at my schedule, it was comical to think that all of those things packed into my week would actually make me less stressed. The reality is you can't *work* your way out of burnout. I know many of us have gotten ahead in pretty much every other area of our life by working hard, but burnout is the opposite. We need to figure out how to do less in order to recover and ultimately be able to do more or sustain what we already have. It goes against everything we've embodied in our lives to get the accomplishments and success we've earned, but the true recovery and lasting change that will keep us healthy and happy long term is actually in surrendering our need for control and allowing the healing in. So often our need to be busy keeps our natural healing abilities from taking over—and that's not something we're meant to control.

Prince Harry and Serena Williams have both been quoted talking about doing "inner work." It's the practice of looking inward to your authentic self and taking time for the things that ignite your passion, creativity, and innovation.[5] It's about constantly checking in with ourselves and building resiliency to help stave off burnout. Of course, this will look different for everyone. For Prince Harry, he realized he needs to meditate every day, while Serena carves out moments of "me time" throughout her day to simply turn her brain off. She stresses the importance of mental health because if you're not healthy mentally then eventually you break down physically, and it's a domino effect from there.

During the height of the pandemic, Starbucks saw how much their employees were suffering mentally. People were showing up late to work, calling off sick, zoning out while on the job, and were generally overwhelmed with everything that was going on in their lives and the world. They knew their team members needed help. So they took action and offered their employees up to twenty therapy sessions per year as part of a sweeping expansion of the company's mental health benefits.[6]

This initiative did two things: It showed their employees that they matter, their mental health was important, and that they were invested in them as a whole person for the long haul. Secondly, because there were twenty sessions included per year, it meant that team members could get the ongoing support that's needed to address their mental health.

Therapy usually isn't a one-and-done thing. As much as we'd love to go to one thirty-minute session and feel 100 percent after, that's not how it works. It takes time and requires us to slow down in order for us to work through what's troubling us so we can speed up and be better, healthier versions of ourselves later.

"Self-care" is a term we hear constantly in reference to burnout. But it's a loaded term that somehow now often means bubble baths, face masks, and wine. Don't get me wrong, all of those things are fabulous and can be a great way to de-stress. But as Fred Luskin, PhD, associate professor at the Institute of Trans-personal Psychology and the director of the Stanford University Forgiveness Project, says, "If you take a bath just to get away from the kids, the minute you open the door, it's like you didn't even take a bath . . . Or how many people take a vacation, and on the plane coming back they're just as stressed? It's attitude and where your mind is, not just what your body is doing."[7] He explains, "You have to consciously practice bringing intention inward, consciously letting go of all the things that worry you, actively kiss them goodbye."

Self-care doesn't have to cost a thing: time off your phone or away from your computer, moments of quiet or meditation, or a walk during the day all cost nothing. It can be something personal and quirky: making homemade masks, putting those old threadbare sweats on, and painting your toes with your favorite song playing in the background.

Self-care can involve someone else. Do something nice for your partner because it makes you feel good about yourself. Do a messy activity with your kid like finger painting or paper mache. It's fun to do something messy as an adult, and because there's no real way to do it neatly, you don't have to stress or micromanage your kid.

Self-care can also be something you don't do, like saying no to evenings out with friends. Not picking up the phone when you know all you'll hear is a monologue from someone complaining about the same issue without actually doing anything. Sometimes sitting on your couch watching trash TV with your dog is exactly what you want to be doing. So do it.

The key is, don't rush. Slow down. Figure out what brings you joy and do that. But prime the pump before you do it. Take a moment before you begin to recognize how lucky you are to do it. Think to yourself, *I'm so lucky to have an hour to myself to aimlessly roam the aisles of Target. I'm so lucky to have twenty minutes to take a bath or a walk, read a gripping novel, cuddle with my kid/partner, whatever.* You get the idea.

Get Shifting Now

Try the Coco Chanel Takeoff

Start by thinking small. Taking steps to let yourself rest and recover from hard work and dedication doesn't have to mean a three-week vacation you plan for months. Slowing down can be cumulative and built through taking small steps each day. It can be small, simple actions incorporated into your daily life that help you find moments of quiet and peace amid the chaos. It doesn't always have to mean taking a vacation.

You may have heard that famous quote by iconic French fashion designer Coco Chanel who says that when dressing with accessories:

"Before you leave the house, look in the mirror and take one thing off." Her point being that *less is more.*

I take the same approach to my schedule each week and call it the "Coco Chanel Takeoff." Every Sunday evening, I review my schedule for the week and find one thing I can remove. Maybe it's a meeting that really can be an email. We all know there are plenty of those! Maybe it's dinner with friends when I've already got commitments four other nights that week. Perhaps it's a facial that could be rescheduled to next week. Maybe it's driving the kids to soccer practice. This might be the week to see if your kid can carpool with another family, and you'll do pickup duty next week.

The point isn't to shirk your responsibilities or just cut all the self-care items. The point is to take a realistic look at your schedule, see which days are heavy with items, know yourself enough to know that you've overbooked, and kindly and politely take one thing off. It works, is addicting, and feels incredible.

Create Quiet Moments

Creating quiet moments throughout your day is imperative to giving your mind and body a moment to relax and preventing burnout. One of my favorite ways to do this is to turn off the music when you're in your car. I'm not talking about that six-hour road trip. By all means, blast that music and sing at the top of your lungs. It's one of my absolute favorite things to do. I always think of my car as my own personal recording studio.

I'm talking about the day-to-day errands we run that put us in our car for ten to twenty minutes—taking your kids to school, driving to work, going to the grocery store, the gym, the dry cleaner, you get the idea. Use those small segments of time throughout your day to just be quiet, let your mind relax, think about how you're feeling, or just simply *be*. Listen to the air-conditioning, the hum of cars around you, roll the windows down and feel the fresh air on your face. Whatever makes you happy.

It will feel oddly quiet and strange at first, but once you get used to it, you will absolutely crave this quiet time. And when you do turn on your radio, it will feel noisy and make you feel overstimulated.

These moments of silence can take many forms—whether it's walking your dog, eating lunch in silence without aimlessly scrolling on your phone, meditating, or sitting on your porch in the sun drinking your coffee. Try scheduling them onto your calendar so that you actually make time for them. As we all know, if it's not on the calendar, it rarely gets done. So take the time to schedule you time every day.

Chris Lindsay, the retired Navy SEAL captain I interviewed, recommends finding other interests. "Find something that really interests you and gets you in a flow state. Those who have this do better. They get perspective from this. Those who don't have anything else, lose their perspective," he shares.

Similarly, Danielle Noble, a partner at a top law firm, says, "Reminding myself on a day when I didn't get as much done as I wanted that every morning is a fresh start really helps. Call it a mantra or meditation. I try to have a gratitude practice every night before I go to bed and every morning when I wake up."

Ask Yourself This Question

On a day when I'm feeling flustered and trying to do too much, I ask myself what I call the golden question: *What is better for my health?*

Here is an example of a day when this trick came in handy: I've got back-to-back calls all day, and I'm having company over in the evening, and I want to tidy things up a bit in the twenty minutes I have between calls. But I also haven't eaten all day, need to take the dog out, and need to get back to all those emails in my inbox. Instead of trying to do everything under stress or skip the meal to clean, I ask myself, *What is better for my health?* and then do that and let the other thing go. In this case, eating a healthy meal and providing my body with the nutrients it needs to keep going is the clear winner.

In these situations, it's easy for most of us to just grab a snack or a sweet. Then before you know it, you're at the end of the day and realize you've eaten nothing but garbage all day. Use the lack of cleaning as an excuse to bust out all those candles and turn the lights down for some ambiance that also hides the dust. Your friends won't care.

It sounds crazy, but just stopping for a microsecond when you're feeling flustered and asking yourself *What's better for my health?* when you're trying to do too much really works wonders in helping you get your priorities in order and slow the heck down so you can speed up later. I've even gone so far as to put a Post-it on my computer that says *What is better for my health?* to remind myself to keep that front and center when I'm making decisions throughout the day.

Pay Attention to Your Body

If we don't listen to our bodies and slow down regularly, they'll force us to. How many times have you heard the story about someone who was seemingly doing it all and then "out of nowhere" they had a heart attack or a stroke or a panic attack that landed them in the hospital? It happens all the time because ultimately there is no such thing as doing it all.

My dear friend Bobbie Singh-Allen, who also happens to be the mayor of Elk Grove, California, has had this happen to her a few times. She says, "I can't help but wonder that when I have a mishap like kidney stones, which I get every few years, that it's my body saying slow the heck down. Pay attention to when your body is rebelling against things. It means you need to slow down."

When I was twenty-five, I got a sharp pain in my chest. It radiated down my back and into my right leg. I ignored it and figured I just pulled a muscle or something and figured it would go away. But it didn't. It got worse. The pain persisted. I felt short of breath and kept having to take really deep breaths just to feel like I could breathe. Naturally, I thought I was having a heart attack, even though I was only twenty-five.

When the pain didn't stop for days, I made an appointment with my doctor. I got blood work done, an X-ray, an ultrasound, did an EKG and a stress test, all the things. And what was wrong? Absolutely nothing! It was all stress induced. I literally thought I was dying, and there was nothing wrong with me except too much stress. This was my first real introduction to how your body processes stress and creates physical problems if you don't look after it.

More recently, my husband and I had been trying to have a baby for years. I'd spent my entire life trying *not* to get pregnant—like being on the pill and using condoms for double protection. I just assumed, like many, that when I was ready to have a baby, I could. How naive.

We tried naturally at first, as one does, but got nowhere. Since I was in my late thirties and my husband was in his early forties, we thought we'd try IVF. As we were older, time was of the essence, and we figured we'd take the most direct path to a baby.

As I laid there on the gurney at 5:30 a.m., naked and cold under the hospital gown, with a thin blanket the nurse gave me to try to make me feel comfortable, hospital-issued socks with the little grip dots on the bottom, and the ever-fashionable hairnet, I was full of hope. This was our fourth round, and I just knew this was going to be the time we would be successful.

After spending nearly $100,000 on treatments, we decided that this would be our last round. It had to work. We were running out of time (and money). If we couldn't get pregnant through IVF, then we were really, truly out of luck in our pursuit of having a biological child of our own. Sure, we could adopt, and every well-meaning person says you'll probably get pregnant as soon as you adopt, but I had, and still have, this deep feeling in my soul of wanting a biological child. I just don't think there could be anything more magical in the world than seeing your own biological child.

They put my IV in, injected me with a cocktail of drugs, and next thing I knew an hour had passed and I was laying in the recovery room with a hot IV bag used as a heating pad on my stomach. I was groggy. The nurse was trying to talk to me, but I was fading in and out of consciousness as the anesthesia slowly wore off. As soon as I came to, all I wanted to know were how many eggs they got. Usually, the nurse tells you right away. But this time she didn't say anything. All she said was that the doctor would be in soon to see me. This didn't sound good.

I waited for what felt like an eternity alone in that empty recovery bay, separated by only a flimsy sheet between me and the person next to me who I didn't see, but heard the nurse tell her that she got thirty-five eggs. *Thirty-five freaking eggs!* That is amazing. I could only hope I would be so lucky.

The doctor came in, and the second I saw her face I knew it wasn't good news. She opened her mouth and all I heard was "three eggs." I didn't hear anything else. I didn't see anything else. My eyes welled up and I started bawling. Because this was during COVID-19, my husband wasn't able to be in there with me, so I just laid there, crying, alone. Alone and empty. Knowing that my dreams of having a baby were over.

Of course, there was a glimmer of hope with the three eggs, but it was minimal. In previous IVF cycles we had gotten eleven eggs and none of them ended up being viable. So, I knew we needed a miracle for one of those three to be viable. Sadly, none of them made it, and after three years our IVF journey was over. I was devastated.

What I didn't realize at the time was that my body was in such a state of depletion from overextending myself at work and excessive stress that it's no wonder I wasn't able to get pregnant. I had done all the right things—the acupuncture, supplements, diet changes, etc., but I still had underlying stress that sabotaged my eggs and hopes of becoming a mother.

Unfortunately for me, my window has likely closed now. This is something I still grapple with—the fact that I may never have my own family. I don't want you to have to go through some version of what I went through before you realize that you need to listen to your body. There are so many small ways we can be conscious of how our bodies are coping with stress. One of the simplest is sleep. Ben Nemtin, *New York Times*–bestselling author and keynote speaker says, "Sleep is huge. It's a sign things aren't going well. My measure of success is if I sleep through the night. If I do, it means I'm not worrying or anxious about something enough to keep me up."

You cannot do it all. You have to take time to rest and relax in order to maintain optimal health and performance. Listen to your body. It will always tell you what it needs and more often than not, it needs rest.

Trap Talk

"When I was younger, I didn't prioritize sleeping as I should have. Getting enough rest or down time. I would just go and go and go. I didn't fully appreciate vacation, time away, half the things that you should be appreciative of and should be doing to reap the rewards of a successful career. I was always focused on the next deadline or promotion." —Danielle Noble, partner at a top law firm

● ● ●

Pausing isn't permanent and doesn't mean that you've failed. It's a necessary part of the process and should be scheduled into your day as a reoccurring meeting. It's only when we truly slow down that we can recharge and refocus to have more energy for what's most important to us.

Slow Down to Speed Up Jumpstart

- **Take one thing off your calendar.**
  Look at your calendar for the week. What is one thing you can remove? Is there a meeting that can be an email? Can your kid carpool to soccer practice one day? Can you move

that dinner to next week? Lighten your load and give yourself space to rest.

- **Turn the music off.**
  Next time you get in your car by yourself, turn the music off. Whether you're heading to the supermarket, dry cleaner, gym, post office, whatever, keep the music off. Give yourself moments of quiet throughout the day. Your mind will thank you.

- **Make a list.**
  Take a few minutes to create a list of the moments when you feel the happiest, most alive, blissed out, relaxed, or in the flow. Then honestly assess if the way you spend your days and weeks is aligned with what brings you most joy? Most likely you will need to make some adjustments. Find ways to incorporate more of those moments and activities into your daily and weekly activities. This won't happen overnight, but if you can slowly introduce more of these into your days, you will ultimately feel more relaxed and aligned.

- **Ask yourself this question.**
  Next time you feel flustered when you're trying to do too many things at once, ask yourself the golden question: *What's better for my health?* Taking a second to ask yourself this question instantly puts things into perspective and helps you make decisions based on what's best for you in that moment.

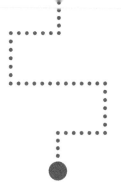

TAKE A VICTORY LAP

Instead of the constant "go, go, go, win, what's-next" mentality, shift to enjoying the moment, showing gratitude, and savoring the wins.

Whether it's keeping up with the Joneses and influencers on Instagram or always focusing on the next thing at work, it's so easy to get caught up in constantly looking for approval or validation by doing or having the next thing. It's also natural to want to move up the food chain—get the bigger house, fancier car, designer clothes, higher-end golf clubs, fly first class, etc. As we know, it's very easy to spend money, but it is a hell of a lot harder to earn it. And often, we just buy and buy thinking it's going to make us happier, but, ultimately, it doesn't.

Psychologists Philip Brickman and Donald Campbell discuss this notion of chasing rainbows and constantly looking for happiness in their seminal work from 1971. They call it *the hedonic tread-mill* and argue that we continue to seek happiness from external events—a promotion, buying a house, finding a partner, having a baby, etc. And while those events may give us a slight boost of happiness, we ultimately settle back down to our base level of happiness once the happiness high wears off. As Type As, we're addicted to the high and pursue it relentlessly.

As motivated, driven people, it's easy to keep plowing ahead constantly thinking about what else you can cross off your list before the day is done. I don't know about you, but I've been known to add things to my list that weren't even on there that I've already done, just to cross them off and make myself feel like I've accomplished more. Fold the laundry? On the list. Empty the dishwasher? On the list. Check emails, make the bed, school drop-off? Check, check, check.

That's why our final mindset shift is to **take a victory lap.** Instead of the constant go, go, go, win, what's-next mentality that can lead us into the Type A Trap and burnout, it requires a shift to enjoying the moment, showing gratitude, and truly *savoring* the wins.

Talking Shift

It's so easy to get caught up in what's next that we can forget to celebrate or even acknowledge what we've already accomplished—even the little, seemingly insignificant things are important. Failing to celebrate the small wins can weaken our self-esteem because we're not acknowledging all the hard work we've put in, our progress, contributions, and discipline. This tendency also trains us to overlook major changes and growth we've traveled through because those tend to be subtle steps forward day after day; this is some of the most important work we do on ourselves in our lifetime, but there is rarely a dramatic waterfall of external success associated with untangling limiting beliefs, healing trauma, and healing our nervous systems. We forget to give ourselves some damn credit for these huge accomplishments that give us more life than any other surface-level habit we're trying to latch onto. Failing to celebrate these accomplishments can also fracture our connection with our higher self since we're so busy plowing ahead that we fail to listen to what we really need—whether that's a new challenge, a break, deeper connections with others, or something else. We can be so focused on moving forward and getting more "done" that we fail to focus on what we truly need or want. All of this can leave our teams feeling unappreciated and us with empty tanks and no time to fill them back up.

A few years ago, one of my best friends was heading to Costa Rica with her extended family, husband, and three young kids. She's always struggled with her weight, and while she was looking forward to exploring the country and making memories with her family, she was absolutely dreading the thought of being in a bathing suit for so much of the trip.

She started training weeks before the trip—anything she could do to tone up and slim down, she did. Going on the keto diet, working out every day, tracking macros, drinking a gallon of water a day, cutting alcohol and caffeine, she did them all. Her list of things she had to do to lose weight, as well as pack everything her family needed for the trip, was a mile long every day.

As the vacation approached, she was feeling a bit better about herself, but still not great. Throughout the entire trip, she rarely wore her bathing suit, was constantly covering herself up with towels and sundresses, and was making excuses to her kids about why she wasn't getting in the water.

As most vacations do, the trip came and went in the blink of an eye. On the flight home the guilt started to set in when her four-year-old daughter asked her where she was when she and her siblings were playing in the waves. Cue the tears. My friend had missed out on so many special memories because she was so fixated on her weight and what she looked like in a bathing suit that her daughter didn't even realize she was on the beach the whole time. Her kids didn't care what her thighs looked like, or whether they rubbed together when she walked, they just wanted their mom to boogie board with them, make sandcastles, and splash in the waves. My friend was so fixated on the end goal of her dream weight that she missed so many small wins on the trip, like the first time her oldest daughter caught a wave on a surfboard, the first time her son went snorkeling, and the first time her youngest daughter floated on her back.

Celebrate Progress

As Type A high achievers, we're always after *something*. Before we even accomplish a goal, we know what the next one is going to be to replace it. We just go, go, go and never reflect on progress or growth. For many of us, the thrill is in setting a goal that seems completely unrealistic and unattainable and then achieving it. So it's natural that as soon as we accomplish one thing, we're right on to the next. The achievement high can be intoxicating, and we are *absolute* addicts! But it's important to stop and acknowledge when we've made progress, especially when we've achieved something we've been after for a while.

A recent study by OnePoll for TGI Fridays found that on average people have four small wins a day or 1,460 each year.[1] These wins can be anything, like scoring a prime parking spot, hitting all the green lights, finding twenty dollars in the pocket of a jacket you haven't worn in a while, decorating for the holidays, discovering a new musical artist you adore, or taking a long bubble bath that leaves you in a deliciously Zen state.

The study, which surveyed more than 2,000 Americans, found that celebrating life's little wins every day goes a long way to improving our outlook on the day and thus, our overall happiness. In fact, 87 percent found small wins to be crucial for powering through the rest of their day, 90 percent said they have a positive effect on their mental health, and 82 percent said small wins are key to having a good day.[2]

Psyched!
Dr. Madelyn Blair

"My experience is that we don't celebrate very well in the United States. Because we have few celebrations, we think we have to do a lot to celebrate. If it's a wedding, it has to be the biggest celebration that anyone ever dreamed of. If it's not a wedding, then we need an excuse to do so. For example, a birthday isn't enough. It has to be a major birthday like turning forty, as if forty is magic. Contrast this to visiting a garden. When you visit a garden, there are flowers everywhere. They bloom just because they are alive. That's what I would like to see in our lives—celebrating just because we are alive."

For me, small wins take many forms, and they vary each day. One day a small win could be eating healthy all day or drinking the water goal I have for myself. Another day, a small win could be exercising my dog enough that he actually gets tired and sleeps for the rest of the day. He's a boxer puppy after all, and damn, do those things have endless energy! And another day a small win could be as simple as changing the sheets or responding to an important email. The key is not to judge yourself but instead genuinely celebrate the small wins. When we complete or accomplish these things, we often get a small ping of pride in ourselves or relief that we've completed the task. Soon after, high achievers will bulldoze the moment because they're always reminding themselves they need to do more, more, more. But when we rewire our patterns to take a moment to appreciate these small steps, balance and happiness follow, which keeps us from falling into the Type A Trap. In fact, 87 percent of the respondents in the OnePoll survey said that recognizing small wins is actually a crucial form of self-care in and of itself![3]

One thing the pandemic taught all of us was that life is precious and incredibly fragile. Our entire lives can change in an instant, and they did. There is no such thing as a win that is too small to celebrate, and one of the best ways to relish in these moments is to tell a friend. Sometimes something as simple as calling a friend and letting them know about your small win can change your entire outlook on your day and put a little extra pep in your step. Find a friend whom you can do this with so that you don't feel lame calling them up and being excited about the fact that you got through all the laundry today. Give yourselves permission to hype each other up about anything the other deems a small win.

As MTV star and keynote speaker, Ben Nemtin says, it's not only important to celebrate the wins thoroughly, but it's important to celebrate the progress that we make along the way and the feeling that goes along with those wins.

A study at Harvard found that celebrating progress is the single most important factor that influences employee happiness. They called it the "Progress Principle." They discovered that the more frequently people experience that sense of progress—or small wins—the more likely they are to be happy and productive in the long run.[4]

When James Watson and Francis Crick were working on discovering the structure of DNA, they went through a roller coaster of emotions before they discovered the double helix, which ultimately earned them the Nobel Prize. Anyone who has worked on a major project can relate. You make some initial progress, feel euphoric, realize that there are still a number of problems, your morale sinks, you doubt yourself, lack motivation, and then you have to dig deep to get your head back in the game to keep plowing ahead. But once they found the double helix and their colleagues didn't find any fault with it, they were elated. Watson wrote, "My morale skyrocketed."[5] Watson and Crick were so encouraged by their progress that they spent long hours in the lab, eager to complete the work. In short, whether or not they felt progress had a direct correlation to their reactions and productivity.

If you are a leader, the Progress Principle suggests that you have more influence than you may realize over employees' well-being, motivation, and creative output. Knowing what serves to catalyze and nourish progress—and what does the opposite—turns out to be the key to effectively managing people and their work.

Early on, the Harvard researchers realized that a central driver of performance was the quality of a person's emotions, motivations, and perceptions over the course of a workday. If a person is motivated and happy at the end of the day, they probably made some progress. If the person drags out of the office disengaged and joyless, a setback is most likely to blame.

When we think about progress, we often think about how good it feels to achieve those long-term goals or experience major break-throughs. Sure, these big wins are great—but they're also relatively rare. The good news, as we've discussed, is that even small wins can boost morale tremendously. Many of the progress events that Harvard's research participants reported were only minor steps forward, yet they often created huge positive reactions.

Trap Talk

Nick Rimedio, the general manager of the W Hotel in Hollywood, talks about taking a victory lap as an opportunity to savor all the things you've worked so hard for. He says, "Whether walking the streets of London or Paris or in a pool in Maui, and you say, 'Fuck yeah, this is why I work so hard.' It's fun to savor those times."

The most important thing to remember about the Progress Principle is that by supporting progress in meaningful work, leaders improve employees' work lives and the organization's performance. So take the time to recognize your team for their hard work, the progress they've made, the milestones they've hit, and the goals they've regularly achieved. It is one of the simplest, yet often underused ways to make your team feel appreciated and supported.

One tactic that's helped me manage my teams more effectively over the years and make them feel appreciated is to have each team member fill out a short survey when they're hired. It asks them to share what fills their tank. It also asks how they like to be recognized (publicly, privately, other), who they appreciate recognition from (peers, managers, directors, executives, customers), and what form they like that recognition in (handwritten notes, food, flowers, certificates, etc.). The form also asks them several things about themselves—favorite foods, sports teams, hobbies, what gives them their greatest joy, and how they measure success. This short survey helps me, as their manager, understand what makes them tick and how I can best support them, and it helps them feel appreciated in the ways that matter most to them.

Positivity without the Toxicity

While it's important to celebrate the progress we make throughout our days and weeks, there are obviously setbacks along the way. When those happen, it's easy to focus on the errors or imperfections. High achievers can be highly self-critical, and it usually doesn't help us bounce back any faster. Supporting ourselves and thinking positively about the momentum we're building is incredibly important and keeps us from getting stuck in a negative thought spiral—which can become toxic and insidious, keeping us from celebrating and growing for months or even years.

To help prevent this, a popular course at Harvard Business School actually goes so far as to teach their students how to manage happiness and the importance of being personally responsible for finding the positive in ourselves and celebrating so that we can affect this change in our teams.[6]

With people leaving their jobs at alarming rates, happiness at work is more important than ever. Companies are scrambling to keep people happy by offering free workouts, expanded benefits, flexible working hours, and more, but is it working? The Harvard professor that teaches the course, Dr. Arthur Brooks, argues that happiness is key to being an effective leader. By regularly focusing on four areas—friends, family, meaningful work, and faith or spirituality—leaders can help their teams cultivate happiness.[7]

The course, which is similar to those also offered at Stanford and Yale business schools, started after Dr. Brooks felt lonely as a leader and knew that many of his fellow leaders did too. It's one of many courses designed to help left-brained high achievers acquire and expand on the soft skills needed to be both a successful manager and a happier manager.[8]

So often, we see high achievers delay gratification, constantly thinking, *When I achieve x, I'll be happy.* But as soon as they do that thing, they're immediately on to the next. Just like the hedonic treadmill, we're constantly searching for that next thing we're going to accomplish, that next happiness high that makes us feel good for a few minutes, hours, or days. This turns into a vicious cycle of not taking the time to actually be happy and enjoy the moment, and ultimately it just feeds into burnout.

Psyched!
Dr. Madelyn Blair

"As a leader, celebrating just because we are alive brings an additional benefit. For example, when you see someone doing something that is done with real excellence or simply done with real passion, it's an opportunity to tell the person what they are doing is valued by you. It can give a person a real lift in their busy day and, at the same time, help them know that their performance is recognized. Additionally, they learn what works and know to do it again—whether they did it consciously or not, whether they were working on it or not, whether they were testing out a new strategy or not. Notice that the recognition had nothing to do with goals. It had to do with day-to-day performance. From experience, I can tell you that it is the most powerful form of celebration when you see celebration as a way to lift the spirit."

I know I've been guilty of this many times as well. Ever since I graduated from undergrad, I knew I wanted to get a master's degree from a first-rate institution. My dad received his PhD from Harvard, and I always was so impressed by that and wanted something similar for myself. Thankfully, he never pressured me at all. But I managed to get into the University of Cambridge in the UK and went on to graduate with honors.

It was rigorous, but so fun. I lived in Cambridge, which is one of the most beautiful medieval towns in England. If you haven't been, you really must add it to your list to visit. I was surrounded by some of the most intelligent, interesting people that I'd ever met from all over the world and was taking classes in the same halls as icons like Charles Darwin, Sir Isaac Newton, Sylvia Plath, Alan Turing, Francis Bacon, and Stephen Hawking. I felt like I was living in a Harry Potter film, complete with wearing gowns and eating lavish dinners in huge, ornate halls . . . but without the spells.

While at Cambridge, I often felt invincible. I was at one of the most prestigious universities in the world, an academic epicenter, working hard and doing well. But even while I was there, I was constantly thinking about what was next—what job I would get, where I would live, who I would meet, how much money I would make. I couldn't totally enjoy it because I was so fixated on *what was next*.

As luck would have it, I went from a euphoric high at graduation to one of the most epic lows I've ever experienced. It was the first time I'd ever had depression. All of a sudden, I found myself at thirty years old, back in California, living with my parents in my childhood bedroom, unemployed, single, broke, and up to my eyeballs in student loan debt. All this while most of my friends were already married, having kids, and owning homes.

It was awful. I was so depressed, but I didn't have health insurance so I couldn't even go to a doctor to get help. I felt trapped, hopeless, and miserable. I had been so fixated on what would come next after I graduated, that when life didn't go the way I'd planned—getting offered an amazing job with ridiculous pay and Prince Charming waltzing into my life—I didn't know what to do.

I failed to see what I'd actually already accomplished. It is no minor event to get into Cambridge, let alone graduate with honors. But I did it. And I met some fabulous friends along the way. But none of that mattered. All I was focused on was what wasn't happening for me now. I had my head buried so far down in woe-is-me land that I couldn't see how many other paths were actually available to me. I would've seen an abundance of opportunity if I just took the time to see it. All I needed to do was stop for a bit, celebrate where I was and what I accomplished, and enjoy this special time with my parents. If I had done that, I would've realized there were so many incredible opportunities just waiting for me.

It took me at least a full year to pull myself out of this black hole. I remember going on walks around my parents' neighborhood, the same one I grew up in, repeating mantras in my head such as, *I'm thankful I'm healthy. I'm thankful I have legs that work. I'm thankful I have parents who love me. I'm thankful I have eyes that can see. I'm thankful it's sunny today. I'm thankful I have food to eat* . . . just the most basic things to be grateful for. But repeating these daily helped me realize I actually had a lot to be thankful for. So much more than so many other people. The importance of celebrating our progress and successes cannot be overstated.

Not only does ignoring our progress to focus on small hiccups keep us from acknowledging our success, but it can also cause us to make more mistakes in the future. Deepak Chopra, author and alternative medicine guru, often talks about how self-doubt derails us as we make progress toward goals. The bigger, more audacious, and longer-term the goal, the more we're going to have to sacrifice to achieve it. And this is exactly where self-doubt, imposter syndrome, and fear of failure can creep in.[9]

On Chopra's website, they define self-doubt as "any thought or belief you have that leaves you lacking confidence in your abilities, skill set, personality, character, or self-worth."[10] We've all been there—feeling like a total fraud, in over our heads and wondering when "they" are going to realize that we have no idea what the hell we're doing. But it's in those moments of pushing ourselves that we get to that next level of growth.

Like almost everything else we've discussed so far, the best way to kick self-doubt is to take action in order to not let it derail us from our goals. Chopra recommends focusing on your strengths and getting excited about the journey you're on, not just the outcome.[11]

Goals aren't meant to be easy to achieve. We're inevitably going to have resistance—both physically and mentally. The key is to ensure our support system is in place, we have the tools needed to push through, and to realize that every step, no matter how small helps us become who we're supposed to be. We can't be so fixated on the result that we fail to see all the progress we've made along the way and enjoy the journey as much as the end result.

Get Shifting Now

Create a Winbox

One tactic that's helped me take a victory lap personally is to create a "wins" folder in my inbox, or what I like to call my "winbox." The higher up you get in leadership, the more it seems like you just get all the problems but none of the awards and accolades. You know what I mean?

We spend so much time supporting our teams, giving them pep talks, making sure they're happy, setting goals, and giving them awards, reviews, training, and bonuses, but those things are rarely done for us. That's why creating a winbox in your inbox can be a game-changer to help you take a victory lap.

Any time you receive a nice email from your boss, a friend, colleague, or family member, drop it in the winbox. Keep in mind that these don't have to be epic, long emails. Sometimes they can be as simple as someone saying, "You've built a great team," or, "Thanks for having my back in that meeting." My former boss was a man of few words and even fewer compliments, so if you got an email from him that said, "Well done," that was a huge win and believe me, that went in the winbox.

After you've amassed a few emails, when you're feeling down and like you need some positive reinforcement, scroll through your winbox and read a few of the past emails. It's such a simple way to remind yourself that you've done good things in the past, people appreciate you, you've had successes, and damn it, people like you!

Schedule Win Meetings

Another great way to make use of your winbox is to schedule weekly hype meetings with yourself at the beginning of each week—intentional time you set aside to reflect on all your great progress and attributes.

This can be as simple as a fifteen-minute Monday morning meeting with yourself to review those emails in the winbox to keep your tank full and remind yourself that you're amazing and you can do great things! The key is to actually put it on your calendar as a reoccurring meeting so that you stick to it.

Now, I realize this is a time commitment, but taking fifteen minutes at the beginning of your week can actually save you time in the long run by keeping you motivated and productive instead of empty and seeking validation through social media, spending money, or through other unhealthy ways.

Send Someone a Win

Let's say you're just starting this whole winbox thing, you don't have any emails in there yet, and you want to get started. The best way to start gathering win emails is to actually send them to others first. If there's someone on your team who's really stepped it up recently, send them an email telling them. If your spouse or partner has been especially helpful or supportive in an area of your life lately, send them a text or an email to tell them. Not only will this exercise help you spread cheer to your circle and make those people you interact with feel good about themselves, but they'll likely respond with something nice about you.

Of course, this should not be an exercise in fishing for compliments. Obviously, only send a win email if you really mean it. But most of the time, people respond to a compliment with another compliment. So, if your winbox is currently empty, start by sending wins to others.

Hang It Up

Let's face it, most people don't really care where you went to college and care even less about seeing your actual degree. But you care. You know how hard it was to fill out the application, get the grades needed to get in, take the standardized tests and all the extra curriculars you had to do to make yourself a better candidate. You know how hard the classes were, how much reading you had to do, and how many all-nighters you had to pull to finish those papers and study for those exams. You know how good it felt to hear your name called and walk across that stage, do the forced handshake, and get your diploma. You know how fun it was to open the mail a few months later when you actually receive your real degree and know that it's now *official* official. No matter what, no one can take that feeling of accomplishment away from you. That's why it's so important to hang that sucker up and put it in a place that you see regularly.

This doesn't need to become a shrine, but put it in your hallway, office, or somewhere that is easily accessible that you can see regularly. Hell, hang it in your garage if that's the only open wall space. Every time you walk past your degree, you will be subconsciously reminded of what you've already achieved and give yourself a subliminal high five and boost of confidence.

But this doesn't only apply to degrees. If there is some other sort of certification or achievement that you're proud of, hang that shit up on your wall! Climbed a mountain? Hang it up. Birthed a child? Hang it up. Got a massive bonus? Put that check on the wall. Whatever it is that you're proud of, that's meaningful to you, and that will remind you of something fabulous that you've already accomplished needs to have a place on your wall to force you to acknowledge your accomplishments regularly—whether consciously or subconsciously.

Trap Talk

"When I'm drained, I feel like I'm stuck. When my work isn't meaningful, I'm not making an impact, or advancing, I dream. It sounds crazy. Not sleep dreaming, but the visioning dreaming. Thinking about things that are bigger, broader, and more exciting helps me get unstuck." —April Hansen, registered nurse and healthcare workforce expert

Create a Living Scrapbook

We've all heard of vision boards and yes, they're great, but have you heard of a happy board? Get yourself a corkboard and hang it in your office, near the desk you work at regularly, in your bedroom, or in a place in your home you see regularly.

Instead of posting all your dream visions on there that may sometimes feel so far from your current reality, print out photos of all your favorite moments and pin them to the board. Think of this as a living scrapbook. Something that can evolve over time. I like using corkboards and push pins because I can constantly add and subtract things as needed.

Print out photos of your favorite people and your favorite places. Add other things like sayings that make you happy, tickets from the best concert you've ever been to, an email that changed your life, your mom's shortbread recipe that makes your mouth water just thinking about it, or something that reminds you of that time you laughed so hard with your best friend that wine came out of your nose. The point is to fill this board up with everything and everyone that makes you happy, makes you smile, and brings you joy.

So often we focus on what we're going to accomplish next that we gloss over the things that truly matter most to us and have brought us immense joy in the past. It's also important to note that you deserve credit for building the beautiful life you're looking at and appreciating. Use this board as an opportunity to relish in all of your happiest memories in one place. Get lost in those memories regularly. Take time to really look at this board throughout the week, smiling at all the happy times. It will be a quick and easy way to flood your body with happy endorphins.

Find Your Brag Squad

It's been beaten into our heads since birth that bragging is bad, narcissistic, and something that isn't looked at kindly. But I call BS on that! It's imperative to our success to be able to celebrate our progress and big wins with people who "get" us. That's why it's so important to find your brag squad—a group of like-minded people who will happily listen to you shout from the rooftops about your success, no matter how big or small, celebrate you, and hype you up. And likewise, you'll do the same for them. We need a group of people that we not only feel comfortable talking about our wins with but who encourage us to share them.

So often, we find ourselves in friend groups with people who are in different stages of their lives or career—the single woman with all married friends, the only one without kids when everyone else already has them, the senior executive when others are mid-level, or the entrepreneur when everyone else has a nine-to-five job.

When your support system is at a completely different level than you—and I'm not saying one level is better than the other—it's hard for them to relate to your successes. We certainly don't need to ditch all our long-time friends, but we need to make a conscious effort to seek out people in a similar stage of life or career as us so we can feel supported.

There are several ways we can find this group. Your local chamber of commerce is a great place to start. They all have regular networking events, and you can meet some amazing people there. Alumni events from your university, adult sport rec leagues, mom groups, single parent groups, church groups, women in business events, entrepreneur organizations, etc. There is no shortage of groups for you to be a part of and many are free. Take a look at Meetup. You'll find damn near any group on there.

When I first started considering speaking as a full-time job option, my husband thought I had lost my freaking mind. He genuinely thought I was having a midlife crisis that I would even consider quitting my lucrative job as a senior executive leading a large team to become a keynote speaker. The problem was, he didn't get what a speaker was, that it was actually *a thing*, and that it could be far more flexible and lucrative than the role I currently had.

I got zero support from my husband and had to pursue it on my own, motivating myself along the way. Thankfully, I knew one successful speaker—Ben Nemtin whom I've mentioned throughout this book—because I had hired him to speak at our company a few times. He told me about an organization called ImpactEleven that helped people become speakers. I signed up for one of their speaker boot camps, and upon arrival on the first day, instantly felt like I had finally found my people. It was such a sigh of relief to be surrounded by people who all had interesting backgrounds, were incredibly motivated, who wanted to become speakers, and many of whom were actually doing it successfully. Now, a few years later, I have come to cherish this group of people. We're spread out all over the world, but they're only ever a phone call, text message, or DM away. I rely on them heavily to talk me off a ledge when I'm feeling overwhelmed, give me guidance when I need help, and shout about my wins when I get a great gig or have a breakthrough. And I am here to support them enthusiastically in any way I can as well.

Being a speaker, on the road all the time, staying in hotels in random cities by yourself can be lonely. But having a group of like-minded people to collaborate, kvetch, and celebrate with makes it so much more fun. Thankfully, now that my husband has seen me go through the process of building this new career and actually getting booked to do speaking engagements, he's finally come around and is supportive. But it's taken years, and I would have been lost without my brag squad of fellow speakers.

Yes, it will take a little time to find the right group and cultivate those friendships, but the important part is to start and make a conscious effort to find your brag squad so you can celebrate promotions, pay raises, publishing your first book, making your first sale, or potty training your kid. Whatever it is, once you find your people, you'll feel so much more understood and supported in your journey and enjoy celebrating each other as a regular part of your friendship.

Brag Better

Whether you work for an organization and you're trying to advance your career, position yourself as a subject matter expert and leader, or you're an entrepreneur trying to grow your business, it's important to be able to talk about yourself and your accomplishments. But most people are uncomfortable doing so and don't have the language or skills to do it in a way that helps them further themselves.

In her book *Brag Better: Master the Art of Fearless Self-Promotion,* Meredith Fineman suggests a number of ways for people she calls the Qualified Quiet—those who are qualified but don't know how to promote themselves—to do so effectively.[12]

Fineman defines bragging as "seeding facts about your work strategically and cohesively to get what you want."[13] This could be as simple as raising your hand in a Zoom meeting, volunteering for a board position, buying the domain of your name and building a personal website to showcase you as a professional, ensuring your

LinkedIn profile is completely up to date, or sharing an article or blog post you wrote with someone who you think would find it valuable and asking them to share it with their network.[14]

The key is to get comfortable sharing your accomplishments in a way that allows you to take a victory lap while boosting your personal brand. One of the simplest ways I've done this is by forwarding win emails from my team and colleagues to my boss.

Any time I got an email from someone commending the work my team did, one of the videos we produced, a new ad campaign we launched, or the like, I forwarded it on to my boss with a simple note like: "Thought you'd like to know that this video/ad campaign/ whatever is resonating with people."

It's basically an "FYI, I'm fabulous" email, but you're not saying it yourself. You're just forwarding on what someone else is saying about you but doing it in a way that makes you look good.

We need to get comfortable sharing our victories with those that can help us move forward in our careers and our lives. But more importantly, realize that when we share our accomplishments and take that victory lap, we inspire others, show them what's possible, and give them permission to share their successes.

• • •

If we don't ever take the time to relish in not only our own accomplishments, but also our teams', then what's the point? Why are we doing all this? Life is meant to be enjoyed, so carve out some time to take a victory lap. You'll never regret it.

Take a Victory Lap Jumpstart

- **Save a win, send a win.**

  Take ten minutes today to go through your inbox and look for any emails that say something positive about you, your team, or your family. When you find them, drop them into your newly created winbox. Better yet, go ahead and forward one to your boss or spouse, depending on what it is, to share the news and politely brag about yourself. Once you're done with that, take a moment to send a win email to someone. Don't over think this and spend too long writing it. Just write a couple sentences praising someone, something they did or thanking them, and hit send. You'll make their day and start the process of saving and sending wins regularly.

- **Frame it.**

  Dig out your diploma, that certificate, or that thing that took a ton of effort that you're incredibly proud of and put it in a frame *stat*! Visit your local Michaels, Target, Aaron Brothers, or local frame shop, buy a frame, and get that thing up on your wall already. Just buy a frame off the shelf. You don't need some fancy custom frame and matting. The point is to just get it up. One simple hack if you have an oddly sized certificates to buy a larger standard frame and then get custom matting to fit your item. It's way cheaper than getting a custom frame. Put it in a spot that you'll see regularly so you can be reminded daily about something fabulous that you've already accomplished.

- **Build a happy space.**

  Order a corkboard and push pins online, hang it on the wall, and get started putting images of all your favorite people, places, memories, and things on that board. Most national drugstore chains like CVS make it really easy to print photos inexpensively. You simply upload your photos to their site, hit submit, and they're printed and ready in less than an hour, and usually for only a few cents each. We don't need gallery-level photos here, my friend. We just need to create a place that makes us happy every time we look at it.

If you want to make an event of it, invite your friends or family members to do the same. Gather the supplies, have them print their photos, and have them over for wine and an evening of creating a happy space.

- **Sign up for an event.**
  Take fifteen minutes out of your day, open up your phone or your computer, and start searching for a group of like-minded people. If you need more successful single friends, fellow moms or single parents, faith-based or spiritual friends, other bad-ass executives, fellow entrepreneurs or a million other options, start the process of finding them. It will take a while to find the right group, and you'll likely cultivate them one by one. So start today!

  And if you're lucky enough to already have a few people in your life who are at the same stage as you, reach out to them and start your own hype group. Even if you haven't spoken to them in a while. They'll be flattered that you want to connect with them again and that you think enough of them to include them in your hype group. Don't over think it. Just reach out and start.

- **Follow this journal prompt.**
  Bust out that journal you bought with the intention of journaling every day but that you haven't used in ages, or simply open the notes app on your phone and write stream of consciousness for five minutes. Answer this question: What is the one thing I'm most proud of from last week? Was it getting all your steps in, getting your kids to school on time three days in a row, killing it in your presentation, having a great interview, leading a successful team meeting? Whatever it is, write it down and give yourself some praise for kicking ass in one area last week. It's important for us to remind ourselves how much we actually accomplish each week and take a victory lap, even if it's just in our journal.

PART III

Keeping Your Shift Together

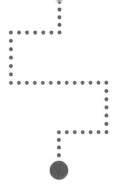

HOW THE TYPE A
TRAP TESTS US

Congratulations on making it this far! I hope by now you've started incorporating the mindset shifts into your life and challenging yourself to take the steps needed to not only heal your burnout, but also to prevent and overcome it. I applaud your efforts and know that it takes courage, time, and commitment to make these changes because altering our inherited and society-driven habits is not easy. If it were, we wouldn't be here today.

Beating burnout is an ongoing battle. As much as we'd love to just take a two-week trip to Hawaii and defeat it for the long haul, as we've discussed, it doesn't work like that. It requires daily, conscious decisions. Our efforts to keep burnout at bay compound in our lives, so consistency is key. Our efforts multiply and ripple outward; the more consistently we practice them, the easier we'll find staying centered.

Just like making healthy choices in diet, exercise, what you watch and read, and whom you surround yourself with demands constant vigilance and effort, preventing and overcoming burnout requires us to make consistent, aligned choices throughout our day, week, and year that move us in the direction of thriving. Because as we've seen, burnout can creep into every area of our lives when we least expect it—from zoning out at work and over delegating responsibilities, to having anxiety, digestive problems, and sabotaging relationships. No area of our life is off limits when it comes to burnout's debilitating effects.

Mitigating and preventing burnout needs to be as top of mind as staying healthy through diet and exercise. We can't just eat healthy one day or work out like a maniac for a week and then be in perfect shape and health. Sadly, it takes daily, constant action for the rest of our lives to maintain a healthy lifestyle. The same goes with burnout recovery. It can't just be something we do while on vacation. Otherwise, we'll spend fifty weeks a year burning out and roughly two weeks trying to recover from it. We might feel slightly better at the end of that "healing period," but we're right back to our same detrimental behaviors once it's over. Sadly, that's a recipe for disaster.

Only through staying on top of it, incorporating the five mindset shifts into our lives, and adopting new, healthier habits will we stand a chance to prevent and overcome burnout and maintain peak performance for the long haul. Our mindsets need to change. And it's okay that we may need to remind ourselves of this and keep relearning these shifts to maintain the healthy balance we deserve.

Beating burnout isn't easy to do. I know that. You know that. That's likely why you picked up this book in the first place. It's hard and takes constant vigilance and determination. If it were easy, we wouldn't have the global burnout epidemic that currently plagues us. We wouldn't have millions of people on Xanax or some cocktail of anti-anxiety and anti-depressant medications. We wouldn't have so many people with seemingly full lives who feel empty, alone, or like they're holding on by a thread to make it all work. We wouldn't have such a thriving industry of companies selling us hope every January to make us think their product or service is the answer to our prayers. It's likely taken years or a lifetime of inherent or culturally engrained behaviors to get us to our current state of burnout, so we can't expect that a quick fix will get us out. We also can't expect that burning out is a one-time thing. Healing from burnout isn't a one-time thing, either.

But don't let these bleak stats scare you. You're putting in the effort, you're taking the steps to heal and prevent burnout. You've now got the knowledge and the tools to break free from the cycle that is leaving so many others struggling. You now know more, so you can do better. I believe in you. I believe in these methods, and I believe in your ability to make the shifts we've talked about.

Burnout will continue to test us and creep in when we least expect it, especially when you first begin your journey. I know how hard it is to reprogram ourselves to not only avoid burnout, but also to pull ourselves out of the spiral when we realize, early or late, that we've been dragged in again. It's taken me years to get to a point where I can recognize the early stages of burnout, and, better yet, where I incorporate anti-burnout habits into my daily life to prevent it in the first place. The allure of the Type A Trap is strong. I naturally love to achieve and accomplish things. It makes me feel good about myself. But when is it enough? It's easy for me to feel a little progress and want more. So I start to get up a little earlier, work through lunch, and work a little later in the day. As the days go by, I can often get to the end of the week and realize that I'm slipping into the Type A Trap. I force myself to take an honest look in the mirror and analyze why I'm craving this external validation of accomplishment. Usually, it's because I haven't worked out much that week, am feeling a little fat, and have had a bit too much wine, so I make up for those feelings of lack by striving to achieve something great that week.

Wanting to achieve great things is not the problem. We all want to do and achieve amazing things in our lives. And we want our teams to thrive. But when those accomplishments come at the cost of your health or you're using them to make up for something else that's lacking in your life, that's when we need to check in on ourselves.

Don't beat yourself up if you get sucked into burnout again and again. It happens and is expected. None of us is perfect. That's why it's called the Type A Trap. It's a *trap*, and it tests us repeatedly.

That's okay, though. Because you get stronger each time you commit to yourself.

Some things in life are seductive, even things that, outside of moderation, aren't good for us. Just like we're constantly tempted by the intoxicating smell of freshly baked bread, mouthwatering sweets, gooey french cheeses, deep dish pizza, McDonald's french fries (and don't tell me they aren't the best), or our favorite wine, burnout will continue to tempt us and lure us in time and time again. Remember, as Type A personalities, we're drawn to the idea of success, and we know how to push ourselves to succeed. It seems too simple to be tricky, but this is how the Type A Trap gets us every time. Even after we've learned its ways.

Just like it's so much easier to stay warm and cozy in bed instead of getting up early to do a workout or go to the gym, burnout will tempt us. It's definitely easier to just eat garbage and not work out, but we all know that is not a recipe for success. We have to eat well and move our bodies regularly if we want to stay healthy, in shape, and live a long, vibrant life. Preventing and overcoming burnout is no different and requires the same sort of ongoing dedication.

But burnout will continue to tempt us with its promise of "just one more thing," "one more accomplishment," "crossing one more thing off the list." It tricks us into thinking getting "there" will bring us that fulfillment we're after, but it doesn't remind us of the cost we pay when we ignore our other needs for rest, balance, and wellness. Usually, as soon as we really start putting effort in to beat burnout, it knows we're giving it less of ourselves and will often fight tooth and nail to keep us there. What follows are a few of the most common ways you may find resistance when trying to beat burnout.

False Sense of Urgency

When we're taking time and backing away from the constant hustle, the Type A Trap has a habit of creating a false sense of urgency inside of us. You may have taken a step back to focus on yourself and implement some of the mindset shifts we've discussed. You're probably feeling at least a bit, or maybe a lot, better and more hopeful for improving your life. Sometimes our tricky minds will only let us enjoy this briefly. The Type A Trap tries to convince us we are running out of time, that we won't be able to attain or accomplish all we want, and, even more frightening, tries to convince us that we may miss out on opportunities, all because we're taking more time for ourselves and away from the grind.

I don't know about you, but I can't tell you how many times I've been working my ass off, burning the candle at both ends, only to finally get to the weekend and instead of relaxing, I think to myself, *Okay, now I can get to all those things on my to-do list: cleaning, grocery shopping, working on my side hustle, laundry, calling my family, cleaning out that closet, filling out that mortgage application, working out, meal prepping, etc.* My weekend ends up being so jam-packed with all the shit I've been putting off because I've been working so hard during the week that Monday rolls around, and I'm not even remotely refreshed. In fact, I'm even more exhausted. And the same thing happens next week and the week after. It never ends!

God forbid I decide to sleep in or lay on the couch and watch a movie for a couple of hours to actually rest. The entire time I'm sitting there feeling guilty that I'm not working on my side hustle, researching, networking, working on my craft, marketing my business, and more. I know I have a few precious hours, so I beat myself up for not using them to further my career and accomplishments. I fear that I'm wasting time and that it's now going to take me even longer to accomplish that thing I have my sights set on. It's honestly exhausting, but it's the truth. It takes every ounce of determination in me to sit still, detach, decompress, and just be.

At work, this false sense of urgency can often take the form of a manager who is constantly in overdrive, pushing their team members because they *desperately* want to cross everything off their list by the end of the day. Therefore, *everything is a crisis.* Everything is a fire drill. Everything must be done immediately. The problem is, if everything is a priority, then nothing is a priority. Teams end up lacking clarity on what exactly they should work on first and feel exhausted, like hamsters on a wheel, unappreciated because as soon as they finish one thing, their manager insists that something else also needs to get done the same day.

Both at home and at work, it takes constant effort to remind ourselves that *resting* is part of high achievement. As I mentioned in mindset shift #4, slow down to speed up, even the world's greatest athletes understand the value of rest and make interval training—an approach that values explosive effort paired with intentional rest periods—a part of their training process. We are no different. We, as high-achieving humans, need the rest too.

We must remember that everything that is truly meant for us cannot *possibly* pass us by. Everything comes in divine timing. It's the old "when one door closes, another one opens" adage.

Growing up, I remember desperately wanting to go to UCLA. I'm from the greater Los Angeles area *originally* (Orange County to be exact), so I grew up being familiar with UCLA and going there from time to time for various things. My cousin got her master's degree there, and I vividly remember visiting her on campus. I thought it was so cool. The campus was massive, in such a fun part of LA, the school had a great reputation, amazing sports teams, excellent academics, and more.

I did well in high school, played varsity sports, had tons of extra curriculars and good grades, but I absolutely suck at taking standardized tests, so I bombed my SAT. I was in all honors classes and got mostly As and a few Bs, but I didn't even get 1,000 on my SATs. And this is back when SATs were out of 1,400. I think I got a 950 or something like that. It was terrible and certainly wasn't what I needed to get into UCLA. Needless to say, I didn't get in, and I was really bummed out. What made it even worse was that people I went to school with got in when I knew full well they had worse grades than me, no sports, and less extra curriculars.

As luck, the universe, God, divine intervention, or whatever you'd like to call it would have it, I somehow stumbled upon a flyer for the American University of Paris (AUP). I applied, got accepted, and by the grace of God, my parents were willing to pay for me to attend. Next thing I knew, I was seventeen and boarding a flight to move to Paris, and my life forever changed.

My time at AUP was truly transformational. To this day, some of my closest friends are those I met at AUP. It was a small, international school set right in the heart of Paris, just a few blocks from the Eiffel Tower. There were only about 750 students there at the time, but we represented more than 100 different nationalities. I studied international communications and political science with the most ethnically and culturally diverse group of students I could have found. To be exposed to such a diverse group of people at such a formative time of my life has absolutely made me the global citizen I am today. It was incredible to learn about the Cold War while sitting in class with students from eastern Europe who lived through it. Or learn about gothic architecture while exploring it on foot in Paris.

I could go on and on about how incredible my time at AUP was, but the point is, when I didn't get into UCLA, I felt like so much had ended. I felt like my hopes of living the life I imagined were over. Like I wasn't destined for the happiness or success I dreamed of. What I didn't realize was that a life even better than I could have possibly dreamed was waiting for me in Paris. Looking back, I'm so thankful I didn't get into UCLA. My time in Paris is forever seared in my heart and opened me up to a world of opportunities and experiences I wouldn't have had at UCLA.[1] Nothing that is meant for us will pass us by. When I was rejected from UCLA, this weight on my chest intensified to figure out my path. But I see now I just needed to relax and allow in an even better opportunity.

So what can we do when this false sense of urgency creeps in? We can start by going back to mindset shift #4 and refreshing our memory on how to slow down to speed up and why it's important. Most of the time, we put arbitrary deadlines on ourselves when it doesn't really matter if we do that thing today, next week, next year, or hell, in five years. Yes, personal deadlines are important, but not at the expense of our sanity and health.

Another thing we can do is put the brakes on any major decisions. I don't know about you, but when I feel like I'm running out of time, I can often make rash decisions that I regret later. I get swept up in a frenzy of feeling like everything has to be done NOW. Everything needs to be bought, scheduled, decided, crossed off the list *now*. It usually doesn't end well. So, the next time you're feeling this way, put a minimum twenty-four-hour moratorium on any major purchases or decisions. Let yourself get out of the mental frenzy, reset, and hopefully make a better decision later.

Remind yourself that nothing you're truly meant for will pass you by, even if you need to take life a bit slower for a while. It is difficult at first, but in these moments when the Type A Trap tricks you into thinking there are urgent matters to get to, regardless of what you need mentally, emotionally, and physically, allow yourself to release that sense of obligation and stress. Your next steps will become clearer in the moments after.

Scarcity Mindset

Much like what happens with the false sense of urgency, the Type A Trap constantly reminds us that there are finite opportunities in the world for us and that the competition is steep. This false narrative combined with inherent Type A tendencies means Type As tend to be hypercompetitive—always hustling, always trying to outdo their peers, and always trying to win.

A scarcity mindset can show up in all sorts of creative and often overlooked ways. At work, it can look like taking credit for ideas and work without sharing the credit with your team or colleagues. Perhaps it materializes as not sharing leads or information that could help your team or gossiping and putting others down to make yourself look better or stand out more.

In your personal life, a scarcity mindset might present as feeling like you're constantly in competition with everyone else, feeling like you have to keep one-upping your peers, resenting other people's success or advancements because you feel like it means you won't get there too, or always focusing on the negative.

Regardless of how it shows up in your personal or professional life, a scarcity mindset will never lead us to a life of abundance and peak performance. If we're always worried about everyone else's success and constantly feeling like there isn't enough to go around for us too, we're going to stay in a fear-based mentality that slowly eats away at us inside and leads us into burnout and the Type A Trap. Not to mention the fact that it will also piss off a lot of people along the way. No one wants to be remembered as someone who is only out for themselves. But living with a scarcity mindset will do just that.

But don't beat yourself up about it. It's natural. Our minds aren't designed to focus on abundance and gratitude, they're designed to help us survive, that's it.[2] Much like a false sense of urgency, a scarcity mindset is based out of fear. One of the most sure-fire ways to avoid a scarcity mindset is to replace it with a mindset of abundance. I know, easier said than done, but it's possible. There are tons of books written on the topic of an abundance mindset, but Tony Robbins, the guru of all mindset gurus, defines it as "the belief that there are enough resources in the world for everyone—and of being grateful for whatever the universe provides."[3] Shifting your mindset to one of abundance will allow you to see quickly that there are infinite possibilities, opportunities, and paths to get where we want and need to go. And just because someone else is succeeding doesn't mean that there is less opportunity for us.

I remember when I first started out as a speaker, I had a colleague who wanted to get into speaking as well. I told her about the speaker boot camp I was going to, and she instantly wanted to join. And while I thought it would be fun to have her there, I also felt like because she had a more senior role than me—and in my mind more experience in a certain field—that she would become a better, more successful speaker than me. We went to the boot camp, and she got introduced to a speakers bureau before me and started booking speaking gigs before me. It was frustrating because I was the one who introduced her to professional speaking, yet I felt that now she was excelling more quickly than I was.

After months of telling myself that any frustration or jealousy I was feeling was only fear-based and coming from a place of scarcity, I finally started to shift my thinking. I stopped comparing myself to her. She has a completely different background, career trajectory, specialty, and story than I do. We speak about different things. We have different personalities and will appeal to different people and organizations. Just because she's getting booked now doesn't mean I won't, and it also doesn't mean that there aren't plenty of speaking engagements to go around for both of us. It's also important to remember that, energetically speaking, when people close to us are experiencing or achieving things we're working toward, it means those things are *closer* to our reality than ever before, not farther.

As soon as I let go a bit and really leaned in to just being myself, embracing my story and expertise, things took off. I started working with many speakers' bureaus, started booking gigs regularly, and really gained momentum with my speaking career.

It took a little mental adjustment from a scarcity mindset to an abundance mindset, but now it's so fun to have a close friend in the same business to compare notes with, collaborate with, commiserate with, ask for guidance and insight from, and just have fun building our speaking businesses together.

Remember the adage "a rising tide lifts all boats"? This is exactly the abundance mindset. When the tide comes in, all the boats in the sea lift, not just a select few. When we succeed, everyone succeeds. And when someone else succeeds, we succeed. It's so easy to forget this and get stuck in the comparison and scarcity loop—focusing on all the things we don't have instead of what we do, but it's essential that we discard that thinking and embrace the abundance mindset in order to combat the constant temptation to fall back into the Type A Trap.

A quick way to create and maintain an abundance mindset is to develop a gratitude practice. I realize this sounds a bit woo-woo, but hear me out. It works. This doesn't need to be some forty-five-minute journaling exercise every morning. It can be as simple as taking one minute before you get out of bed in the morning to thank the universe, God, or whatever you're into for three things you're grateful for each day. Show gratitude for having a warm, comfy bed, for not having an 8:00 a.m. meeting, for getting to see your parents this weekend, for waking up to a clean house, or actually sleeping through the night. These don't have to be huge, life-changing things. In fact, when we focus on even the smallest things we're grateful for in our life, we find even more things to be grateful for. Our gratitude literally multiplies once we start focusing on it.

Try this out for a week and see how you feel. Taking even one minute each morning to ground yourself in gratitude for what you have can go a huge way to keeping you in an abundance mindset and out of a negative scarcity mindset and the Type A Trap.

Sudden Need for Control

Letting go is not something us Type As are comfortable with. When we release our constant hold on directing our lives and influencing every outcome, our psychology feels a bit off-kilter and will kick back with an aggressive need to control situations.

We've learned through habit that to get where we want to go, we need to micromanage every aspect of our lives. Although this habit can produce results and help us get to great levels of success, as we discussed in mindset shift #2—release the reins—it also dumps us into burnout pretty quickly.

Releasing control is still something I wrestle with daily. I can't tell you how many times I've gotten mad at my husband for not doing something around the house, but then also gotten annoyed with him that he didn't do it "right" when he finally gets around to doing it. I then end up just doing it again myself. He gets mad at me for being controlling and micromanaging him, I get annoyed with him, and the whole cycle continues again the next time.

If we don't want to do everything ourselves, then we have to give other people grace, realize that there is more than one way to do something, that it's not going to be done exactly as we would have done it, and let it go. Done is better than perfect. And if we want to have everything perfect, then we're going to burn out doing it all ourselves.

This need for control also shows up at work in the same way. We often resist or delay delegating tasks because we think if we don't do it ourselves, it won't be done right. Or we know that we are the ones ultimately responsible for the task and don't want to get in trouble for it not being done right, so we avoid delegating and just do it ourselves.

Just like in our personal lives, if we don't ever delegate, teach our team members how to do a certain skill or task, and never give them an opportunity to do it (in an exhibition match for example, like we talked about in mindset shift #2), we're not only holding back their growth, but we're also burning ourselves out along the way.

Our constant need to control zaps our energy. We're simply not meant to control and predict and drive every part of our lives. And that's okay. Doing that takes the fun and spice out of life. We need to understand when it is best to let go of the reins and let the universe take control. When we do this, we will be surprised to see that what manifests was never in our idea for the future, but the reality was better than we thought it would be. We have more energy and vitality after allowing things to come to us, and burnout melts away quickly.

Whenever we find ourselves ruminating or obsessing over a particular outcome or circumstance, take it as a sign that we need to practice releasing and allowing. There are both mental and physical things we can do to move in that direction—from the more woo-woo, metaphysical options of visualizing, note burning, reiki, or affirmations to the more tangible of journaling, yoga, meditation, or massage. The point is, there are options. And your choice may depend on what it is you need to release. Sometimes journaling may help and for something else, a hot and sweaty yoga class may be what's needed.

One of my favorite ways to let go is something I learned in yoga. Lay down on your back. Pull your knees up to your chest and curl up into a ball. Think about what it is you want to release as you curl up into the tiniest ball you possibly can. Tense up every single part of your body and hold it there for a few seconds. Then, let go of your breath and your legs and just lay down with your arms and legs stretched out. Imagine that thing you were holding on to just floating away as you release all the muscles in your body.

There's something about the tension between holding on and tensing everything up and then just letting everything go that makes it really feel like you are releasing whatever pent up, negativity or stress you have in your body or mind.

However you prefer to release, we need to get in the habit of letting things go so that we stop controlling everything and perpetuating our cycles of burnout. Be kind to yourself. Remember that, especially with major life events or stressors (including trauma), you may need to release the same thoughts over and over again. Just because you keep confronting it doesn't mean the practices aren't working or that you're not healing.

Panic and Anxiety

An important aspect of this work of staying out of the Type A Trap is to realize that it can bubble up seemingly unrelated panic and anxiety. Many of us have dysregulated nervous systems from being so vigilant in every area of our lives. So, quite literally, our bodies don't understand what it feels like to just be and relax, which, as we've discussed in mindset shift #4—slow down to speed up—is a key component to beating burnout.

As a speaker, avid traveler, and someone who has taken thousands of flights in my life, sitting on an airplane is something I'm very used to. When I was thirty, I boarded a flight like any other. I patiently sat in the waiting area of the airport until my boarding group was called, jiggling my foot, trying to read, but really just staring at the interesting assortment of people that streamed by. Aren't airports the best places to people watch?

Finally, my group was called, and I filed through the jet bridge into the plane. As I made my way down the aisle looking for 16A, I started to feel warm. I didn't think much of it, as it's always either sweltering or subzero on planes—there never seems to be any in between. I figured it was just warm because we were sitting idle at the gate.

I had never really been bothered about whether I was on the window or aisle. Obviously, no one wants to sit in the middle, but aside from that, I really didn't care where I sat. I muddled down the narrow aisle of the packed plane and got to row 16. I had the window seat, and the two other seats were already taken. As my row mates got up to let me in, I felt sweat drip down my brow and my heart start racing. I tried to brush it off, but something was definitely happening to me.

As I got myself situated and put my bag under the seat, I ripped off my sweater and started fanning myself with the safety manual. I could feel my heart racing, sweat oozing out of every pore, and my eyes started welling up with tears. I didn't know what was happening. It was like something was taking over my body.

I stood up in my seat, and said I had to get out. Keep in mind this was exactly two minutes after I sat down. I made everyone get up again and let me back out into the aisle . . . in the way of everyone else that was still trying to board the plane. Looking back now it was a classic panic attack. But at the time, I'd never had one before and didn't know what was happening.

I asked the flight attendant if there was an aisle seat available and she said no. I asked the people around me if anyone would switch with me, and they all said no. I burst into tears at this point and said I could not sit in my seat and had to have an aisle. Needless to say, I felt absolutely ridiculous crying in the middle of a packed plane for no apparent reason at thirty years old, but I couldn't control myself. It was a full-on out-of-body experience. I wasn't in control of my body.

Eventually, the flight attendant made an announcement and asked if anyone would like to swap their aisle seat for a window one and some lovely gentleman came to my rescue, and I was able to survive the rest of the flight. To this day, I only fly in the aisle seat.

The sudden and intense onset of panic throws many people off, because it usually finds seemingly unrelated moments to surface. Or at least it may seem that way. You could be enjoying a moment with friends or family, and a panic attack strikes. Or like me, it could pop up unannounced on a routine flight you've taken a million times. Nothing that day may be particularly stressful for you, but you fail to notice that for months on end you have been battling anxious thoughts and physical manifestations of stress, all of which decide to release in the moments when you least expect them.

When these bubble up after you make the conscious decision to battle burnout, it can feel like you're failing and that the journey ahead is much steeper than you thought. It is difficult in the moment, but know that these experiences are your body and mind's way of fighting conditioning that is years and sometimes decades old.

Regular, mandated, or scheduled relaxation time is necessary to surpass this hurdle in beating burnout. The key here is consistency.

Make a list of things you know relax you (baths, certain types of music, walks outside, reading a real book not a screen, doing crafts, meditating, cuddling with your dog, talking with a friend, taking a yoga class, getting a massage), and schedule them into your calendar as you would a meeting with a new employer or dream client.

Only through frequent, planned periods of relaxation and regularly doing things that calm our nervous system and bring us joy are we able to keep burnout at bay. It will constantly keep knocking on our door, luring us in. It's up to us to be diligent about keeping our panic and anxiety in check by scheduling "me" time in every day. Even five to ten minutes here and there throughout the day will make a huge difference.

•   •   •

Climbing our way out of burnout is not a simple or straightforward process. If it were, we would all be living at our absolute blissful peaks, and burnout would not be the buzzword of the moment or the global problem it is today. Like anything worth doing, it takes practice, determination, commitment, and consistency. Just like pursuing a healthy lifestyle, preventing and overcoming burnout requires adopting healthy daily habits like we've discussed in the five mindset shifts.

It's likely that you will confront the resistances mentioned in this chapter at various intensities throughout your life, usually in the most unexpected ways or inconvenient times. The goal is to get better at identifying when we're headed in the wrong direction to avoid being completely consumed and lost inside of the burnout black hole. And, more importantly, to have an entire arsenal of tools at our disposal to use in combating burnout in its various stages. Remember, you have everything you need within you to overcome any of these challenges.

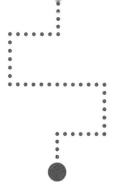

TYPE A TRUST: EMBRACING OUR DRIVE FOR SUCCESS AND NEED FOR PEACE

Being a Type A personality, a high achiever, and a doer is *not* a flaw. It's what makes you the fabulous person you are and has likely been an incredibly important factor in what's gotten you to the level of success you currently enjoy in your life. We are driven, agile, resourceful, and motivating.

There are many aspects of the Type A personality to be proud of. It just so happens that being Type A also makes us a bit more susceptible to burnout. But thanks to the five mindset shifts and tactics we've discussed, it's absolutely possible to be a healthily balanced Type A person—someone living a life with structure and drive but who knows how to check in with themselves and stay aware of their highest priority: their mental health, peace, and wellness. Rest assured that you now have everything within you to climb your way out of burnout and avoid it or lessen its effects moving forward.

Some of the most successful people in history have been Type As. If you watched the 2019 Netflix documentary *Homecoming,* about Beyoncé, you saw her laser-like focus and dedication, her months of rehearsals and practice for her two-hour headlining set at Coachella that turned into a cultural movement. But that's the same Beyoncé who also canceled multiple shows due to exhaustion and even took the entire year of 2011 off to focus on her mental health.[1]

If you read the biography of Steve Jobs, the founder of Apple and Pixar, or saw the movie about him starring Ashton Kutcher, you know how maniacally focused he was on perfection and his vision for his iconic products. You also saw firsthand how these traits wreaked havoc in his personal life. He was short with his team and loved ones, demanded absolute excellence, and accepted nothing less than perfection. He regularly lost his temper and reamed out his team, business partners, and even family and friends. Unfortunately, he failed to find the balance between his focus on achievements and his relationships and health.

If you're a tennis or sports fan, you've likely heard that Serena Williams, arguably the greatest tennis player of all time—male or female—recently retired, or as she calls it "evolved away from tennis," to find more balance in her life. Call it what you like, but even Serena, the winner of twenty-three Grand Slam singles titles, isn't immune to the pressures of burnout. She provides a great example of someone who likely saw the change in tides of how she was feeling, and she decided to make a healthy choice for herself and leave her sport on a higher note than if she kept pushing and abused her mind and body.

Like Serena, the former New Zealand prime minister, Jacinda Ardern, also resigned during the height of her popularity and career stating that she "no longer had enough in the tank."[2] During her tenure, she dealt with the pandemic, a terrorist attack, and a natural disaster on her home soil. This stress, combined with the day-to-day pressures of the job, constant travel, and being away from her young daughter (whom she gave birth to while in office) all eventually became too much for her. She stepped down in January 2023, called for a general election, and said she was looking forward to being home to take her daughter to school and finally marry her long-time partner.

There is no shortage of other examples of well-known people who are successful Type A personalities who have also taken a step back at one time or another to focus on their mental health. They've all had to learn how to incorporate mental health and anti-burnout practices into their lives to keep them at peak performance. And you can do the same.

The beauty of having a Type A personality is that you have achievement potential and strengths that many others do not. But it's possible to honor your inherent nature while turning away from the impulse to only concentrate on achievement instead of looking at yourself as a whole person. The key to this is connection with yourself. Make yourself your highest priority and what you should and shouldn't spend your energy on becomes very clear. Build this awareness, and you're well on your way to a successful, balanced life that feels good and nourishes your whole self. What follows are ways you can continue to honor your authentic, high-achieving self without burning out.

Reevaluate Your Definition of Success

Quite often, our definition of success isn't really something we think about. We just inherently know what it is we consider successful and what it is we don't. But it's important to really question how we are defining success and why that definition resonates with us. Type A personalities are driven by success, so this definition has very real implications on how we behave and how we treat ourselves.

Do the qualities or characteristics of that definition of success have any intrinsic meaning for you? Or are you assuming building a life that looks like someone's on Instagram is what will bring you that happiness? Are we living a life that looks successful to our parents, our partner, or our friends, but makes us miserable inside? Why are we holding onto this vision? Is it contributing to our burnout? After I burned out, I had to let go and reevaluate my definition of success to make room for a new, healthier version of myself.

For as long as I can remember, I've defined success and my sense of self-worth by my accomplishments and productivity. This started at a young age. I grew up with an older brother who was a year ahead of me in school. Not just any older brother, but THE guy that every girl was in love with and every guy wanted to be. He always had a girlfriend; always dated the hottest, most popular girls at school; won best looking in the yearbook; had his pick of any girl he wanted to take to dances—he had all the things that seem really important while growing up.

Me on the other hand, I did not. No one, and I mean *no one,* was interested in dating me. Out of four years in high school, I was only asked to a dance once. One time! I did have a couple of boyfriends here and there, but in general, I felt like my older brother's invisible little sister who was not blessed with his good looks.

On top of that, my best friend since fourth grade (who still happens to be my best friend) was a knockout. Every guy wanted to date her, and no matter what party or bar we went to, all eyes were on her. Guys would come up to me, but only to ask about her. They were definitely not interested in me.

I was getting hit on all sides by feeling like I was the ugly duckling who no one was interested in. Since I didn't feel like I had the looks compared to them, I quickly found my sense of self-worth in my accomplishments. Now, I've always had a very outgoing, strong personality, but my Type A, overachiever, doer personality really kicked into high gear during high school, and more than twenty years later, it has never really stopped.

In high school, I made the varsity swim team my freshman year, was on the dance team, was a cheerleader, took all honors classes, worked a part-time job, and even went to the local junior college at night to learn Italian. In college, I always took extra units each semester as well as summer school so that I could graduate early. Why was I in such a rush? Who knows? But it made me feel good to know that I would finish university in three and a half years instead of four or more like so many of my friends.

Of course, I also hustled to get internships each semester so that when I graduated, I was set up for success in finding a job. In my first few jobs out of college, while establishing myself and working my way up the corporate ladder, I never stopped—working, networking, taking courses to learn more, taking on more respon-sibility, staying late, you name it. I literally spent decades working harder than everyone I knew. In my mind, there was nothing I couldn't achieve if I just worked a little harder.

But after I burned out, I realized that I had to reevaluate my definition of success. I couldn't just keep pushing, doing, and accomplishing at the cost of my mental and physical health. After all, my definition of success is what had left me in the Type A Trap in the first place.

It took some time, a little therapy, and a lot of soul searching, but I was able to come up with a new version of success—one that didn't just measure my accomplishments. Today, success to me is rooted in how I feel. I ask questions like: Have I been working out regularly, do I feel strong, am I eating well, am I in good health, do I spend quality time with my parents each month, am I making time to be present with my husband, do I have strong friendships, am I pursing my passions and things that make me happy, and more? Because ultimately, what's the point of having tons of success but no one to share it with or terrible health so you can't enjoy it?

I still wrestle with it every day, since my inherent Type A tendency is to achieve at all costs, but now I make conscious decisions to measure success by my happiness, health, flexibility in my schedule, how much time I'm able to spend with my family, and a number of the other things.

By redefining success, I've been able to let go of the old me to make room for the next me, and I invite you to do the same. What version of success are you holding on to that may be holding you back and leading you into burnout? It's never too late to redefine what success looks like to you.

Taking time to discover what our authentic selves truly see as success alleviates much of the toxic mindset we've taken on in our pursuit of "success" over happiness and contentment.

Use Envy as Energy

One way to help us reevaluate our definition of success is to use envy as energy. We're told time and again that we shouldn't compare ourselves to other people and shouldn't envy others. It's unhealthy. Hell, it's even one of the seven deadly sins.

But the truth is, envy can be incredibly motivating and just what we need to move to the next step of our life or career. After all, no emotions are bad. We shouldn't feel ashamed of having jealously or envy bubble up during an experience—we should be interested in why that feeling came to the surface. It is trying to guide us toward something. So instead of thinking of envy as something negative, we need to shift our thinking to view it as data on what we value and use those comparisons as a catalyst for change.[3]

I know we've all felt envious. Some of us more than others. Maybe there's someone on social media you don't know but you follow who appears to have this incredible digital nomad life that you envy while you're always stuck at the office. Maybe you have a cousin or an uncle who retired early and is living the dream. Perhaps there's a girl from high school whom you're still friends with on Facebook but haven't spoken to since high school; she seems to have the perfect husband, house, and 2.5 kids that you so crave. Whatever it is, take note of whom you envy and what exactly it is about their lives that you desire. These are all clues and pointers in the direction of your next move and definition of success. Keep in mind that we usually covet aspects of someone's lifestyle not because we want that thing, but we want how that thing will make us *feel*.

A Harvard study came up with something called the *personal envy lab*—a three step process—as a way to help people work through, process, and make sense of envy.[4]

Here's how it works. Whenever you're feeling envious, open up the notes app on your phone and type out what it was that triggered you. Was it something on the news or social media? Was it a rejection? Did someone accomplish something you secretly wished you could have? Writing this down gives us direction and saves us from diving into a negativity spiral.

The next step is to ask yourself what exactly you're envying and what you can do about it. It's about decoupling the person from the attribute. So, for example, let's say you own a construction company, and one of your competitors keeps winning deals instead of you even though you know you're more qualified and do better work. Instead of just being envious that they keep winning deals, reframe it to, *I'm envious of [company]. They're doing a better job of conveying their value to prospects. So, what can I do about that?*

Can you refresh your website? Include better before and afters or more testimonials from clients? Maybe you need to follow some of your craftsman around and put video of their incredible work on your site to really show off the quality of their work. Perhaps you're a third-generation family-owned company, and you need to do a better job of conveying your story and generational commitment to excellence. The key is to figure out how you can let your competitor's success inspire you to get better.

Sometimes, we spend all our time being envious of a person, internalizing everything, and compromising our peace of mind instead of taking action and making the emotion work in our favor.

The last step is to ask yourself, *Would I trade places with the person I am envious of?* A lot of times we only envy a certain part of other people's lives, not their entire existence. Those are the parts to focus on that can spur us on to action and help us redefine what success looks like to us.

Identify an Objective Measure of Growth

As Type As, we have a habit of taking on ill-defined success metrics, many of which can't actually be tracked or objectively observed. We often create arbitrary deadlines for ourselves with invisible, nebulous, and obscure measures of success that don't make any sense to anyone but ourselves.

We'll convince ourselves that we're lazy if we don't write at least fifty pages of our book/paper/report today. That our business is never going to succeed unless we post on social media three times a day. Or that we're fat, even though we work out regularly, eat well, and haven't gained more than a pound in ages. You get the idea. We make up all sorts of terrible stories about ourselves, our lives, and our self-worth based on nothing more than some ridiculous measure of success we've created in our head.

Hilary Rushford, one of my favorite people to follow on Instagram about burnout, business, and life, posted about finding an objective measure, and it really stuck with me. She argues that regardless of what we're trying to measure, we need to find an objective way to measure it so that our warped sense of what is enough doesn't come into play. It keeps us honest with ourselves. For example, you might think you're fat. But the scale doesn't lie. If you actually get on the scale, and you haven't gained any weight from the last time you weighed yourself and you weigh a normal amount for your height and age, you're not fat. You might think you're lazy and beat yourself up because you haven't done the ten million things on your work to-do list for the day. Side note—NO ONE would be able to do all that in one day! But if you were lazy, your business wouldn't be succeeding, your revenue wouldn't be up year over year, you wouldn't have just landed that new client or great testimonial, or you wouldn't have gotten that bonus or promotion at work.

Personally, I know with my own mental health challenges and growth, I lose perspective quickly when my day doesn't go perfectly. Two weeks previously, I may have been anxious every day and really struggling. Then, I may have several good days and maybe a few hours sprinkled in with some intense anxiety, and my mind convinces me no progress was made. How many times have you let one small thing going wrong ruin your whole day or week? We're all guilty of it. We're so quick to throw out all the amazing things we did and accomplished just because one thing didn't go as planned.

By keeping a mood log that captures how I feel each day or part of each day in my calendar, it keeps me honest with myself and shows me that I *am* making progress and healing. My mind just likes to try to trick me that I'm not, so I stay in that scarcity, Debbie-Downer mindset. It also enables me to see trends. If I have too many days in a row that I rate poorly, I know it's probably time to check in with my therapist or schedule some time away from work to recalibrate.

It is important that we get out of our own heads and establish a foundation outside ourselves for evaluating our success. Otherwise, we'll just keep moving the goal post, adding more obstacles that we need to overcome and achieve before we actually succeed in our heads. We're simply sabotaging our happiness perpetually by not using an objective measure of success. And who wants that? Let's find more happiness in life instead of more ways to convince ourselves that we aren't succeeding. The world will do a good enough job of that on its own.

Create a Life outside of Accomplishment

It's difficult for Type As to detach areas of their life from growth, forward movement, and achievement, but it is necessary. Well-rounded lives that feel good, not just ones that look good, have space and ease built into them. It doesn't mean that we'll never feel anxious, get stressed out, or burn out. Of course, that will happen. We live in a crazy world with constant pressure. It just means that we now have the tools to prevent and overcome burnout and the know-how to build those tools into our daily lives so that when we do have stressful situations come up or busy times creep in, we can better address them without falling into the Type A Trap. Creating a fun, beautiful, nurturing life outside of accomplishment is a game-changer to keeping our minds clear and ourselves out of the Type A Trap.

My husband is constantly on my case because, according to him, all I talk about is work. As you can imagine, I don't agree with his assessment, but I'm sure there is some truth to it. I can't help it. I get excited about the things I accomplish, the progress I make, and the milestones I hit. I want to shout about them and celebrate them. I'm a passionate person, and I put my heart and soul into everything I do. If I didn't care that passionately, I wouldn't do it. So that means when I accomplish something, I'm *thrilled*. But I have learned over time that not everyone cares about or is as excited about my accomplishments as I am. And as we discussed, we may need to redefine our idea of success not only for us, but for those around us and the sake of our relationships. I'm not saying abandon who you are and completely change yourself for someone else. I'm saying that a few adjustments go a long way in maintaining our sanity and relationships.

I'm still working through this and am by no means fully "there" yet, but I've found that building in time each week to connect with my husband by getting out of the house and doing something active that we both enjoy is a great way to shut myself up about my accomplishments and build shared experiences together outside of work. Staying intentional about being in the moment and not discussing work or plans in the future or events from the past is particularly helpful.

Different people need different amounts of space and time to connect with themselves, but we all need it. I'm an extrovert, but because I'm such a high-energy person, I need an equal amount of quiet, alone time to recharge, otherwise I turn into a raging a-hole. I can feel myself get testier and testier when I go for long periods without any alone time. It's not healthy. Everyone needs time to themselves.

It is important to build in time for hobbies, connection, and to just *be*. This could be reading, painting, working out, playing or listening to music, time with your pets, volunteering, or dedicated time to sit with your partner or friends and just talk and laugh over a glass of wine. Oh, the joys I've had laughing my ass off with friends over wine. It is truly some of the best soul medicine out there.

More importantly, when we take this time for ourselves, we need to pay attention to how we feel and what we're thinking about. This will foster true connection with your higher self and make you feel more centered and confident in the choices you make.

There Is No True Destination

It is hard for us to remember that life is so much more than our five- or ten-year plan. It's more than just getting through a period or phase. Getting to that next step—getting married, buying a house, having a baby, getting a raise or promotion, or retiring. It's more than hitting that next milestone or taking that next vacation. We are always *getting* somewhere or looking at the *next* goal. But it is important to remember that isn't the point of life. Life is right now, in this moment. And we're missing it if we are always focused on where we want to be and not where we are.

The point is the journey. The point is the constant learning about ourselves and how we can grow into our authenticity. The destination changes and evolves as we grow and our desires and priorities change. That's normal. But if we're constantly just focused on the goal and the destination, we miss all of the truly magical small moments that happen in our lives every day. Often, we also tell ourselves we'll be happy "when…" We'll be happy when we get the job, when we find the partner, when we make the money.

As they say, the days are long, but the years are short. We cannot spend the precious few years we have on this planet wishing our lives away. Wishing for that next step, wishing it was the weekend, wishing our kids were out of diapers, wishing it was spring break, wishing our vacation didn't end, wishing we lived in a bigger house, wishing we had a better job, more flexibility, whatever. What is it that you're wishing for? And is that wish getting in the way of you enjoying your life right now?

Aspiring is not a bad thing, and we should continue to call our shot and get excited about where we can go. However, to avoid burning out and losing ourselves in the fire while we're on the road to that achievement, we need to stay present, grateful, and aligned in the moment. We need to honor the time and space we're in right now. If we don't, we're never going to live the life sitting right in front of us.

One simple thing that's helped me remember to stay present is to take a social media break. A recent study out of the University of Tennessee at Chattanooga shows that after scrolling social media, the biggest emotion people feel is envy.[5] It's no wonder. When all we're seeing is everyone else's highlight reel, it's easy for us to feel less than and wanting something else. Whenever I start to feel the spiral start, I take a short break from social media—usually a day or two, write down the top three to five things I'm grateful for, and remind myself how lucky I am to have those things in my life as well as how far I've come in the last year or so. It gives me perspective and helps me appreciate everything I have and where I am right now.

• • •

We've been on quite a journey together. We looked at what burnout is, its effects in our lives, and how it's sweeping the world. We assessed where we are on the burnout spectrum at the moment and what the warning signs are for each level of burnout. We learned about the intricacies of Type A behavior—the good and the bad. We dug deep into the five mindset shifts that are essential to implement to prevent and overcome burnout. We developed a playbook of tactics to implement for each mindset shift so that we're equipped with the tools we need to stay on track and out of the Type A Trap. We've examined the ways the Type A Trap will test us throughout our lives and how we can combat those tests. We've acknowledged that this process is ongoing, and we'll have to check in on ourselves throughout our lifetime. And lastly, we've discovered ways to maintain a life without burnout so we can stay at peak performance for the long haul.

Whew. It's been a lot to digest, but we got there. It's not easy to take an honest look at ourselves and realize that we need some help in preventing and overcoming burnout. I know what courage it takes to take these steps, and I want to congratulate you for making it this far. You are now equipped with all the information and tools you need to start making some positive changes in your life to keep you out of the Type A Trap, free from burnout and living the life you know is possible.

• • •

There's one more story I want to share with you that really demonstrates how these five mindset shifts can help us not only pull through dark periods of burnout but go on to absolutely thrive as peak performers on the other side:

It was three in the morning, and Nick was wide awake—in a cold sweat, heart racing, tears streaming down his cheeks. His wife was asleep next to him, completely unaware of the silent panic attack he was having thinking about their dwindling bank account, all the bills that needed to be paid, and the implosion of his company that felt like a train wreck happening in slow motion right before his eyes.

This wasn't his vision though: to lose it all, be in such a desperate state, and get annihilated by the media. He had always found a way to make things happen. He wasn't one of *those* people. Never! Yet here he was having the same thoughts I was, except much more severe and on a public stage. At least I had the "luxury" of breaking down in private. He desperately needed a way out, a solution, something to combat the Type A Trap he'd fallen into.

It wasn't always this way though. Just a year earlier, he was the head of an incredibly popular three-billion-dollar company with an industry-disrupting product and was a media and investor darling. But let me take you back to the beginning.

You see, Nick never wanted a real job. When he graduated from college, he gave himself until he was thirty to invent a product and create a successful company. If he couldn't do it by then, he'd get a real job. The fear of having to work for someone else in some windowless, cement-grey cubicle under fluorescent lighting fueled him.

Sadly, his first company failed before he could even launch it. His second company, however, did so well that investors practically begged Nick to take their $3.9 million in start-up money. But two years later, the company went bust and he lost everything.

He took the failures personally and knew he needed to figure this entrepreneur thing out and ask himself some hard questions. And the best place he knew to do that was on a surf trip. So, he grabbed his buddies and headed out on a five-month surf trip around Australia and Indonesia.

A few weeks into their trip, Nick and his buddies were sitting on a beach having just come out of the water and some of the most epic waves they'd ever surfed. They dreamed of becoming pro surfers but struggled to capture their moves on camera to submit to competitions. They never got the shots, but Nick got an idea for his third business.

He borrowed some money from his parents, sold shell necklaces he bought abroad for extra cash, and in 2002 GoPro was born. He introduced the first wearable camera on the market that adventure-seekers could strap to their heads, boards, vehicles, whatever to get the perfect shots of them in action. As you may know, it was an instant success.

I would imagine that many of you have a GoPro. And I don't know about you, but every single person I know that has a GoPro is obsessed with it and has made me watch countless hours of video.

Growth was dramatic, and surfers snapped up every product he released. Four years after it started, GoPro had thirty-five million dollars in annual revenue. And in 2014 when GoPro went public, Nick became an instant billionaire with wealth over three billion dollars.

He was the highest-paid CEO in America and was living large. He bought a yacht, a private jet, homes all over the country, and a fleet of vintage sports cars. He was working one-hundred-hour weeks to push the company forward, to keep it alive. But two years later, all that spending, the long hours, constant grind, and exhaustion caught up with him and sent him into the Type A Trap—becoming his and GoPro's undoing.

This is when Nick spiraled into the deep depression I mentioned earlier. How did he bounce back? He followed the Type A mindset shifts and rebounded to be the company we all know and love today and that I drive past almost every day in San Diego.

Just as we heard in mindset shift #1, his first step was to **decode his flow** and get back to his passion. He had chased this red herring of thinking that everyone wanted to watch videos of other people on adventures, so he got deep into the media and content creation business, but the truth is people wanted to create their own epic videos and be the heroes of their own stories, so he decoded his flow and went back to what made GoPro popular originally: creating the best wearable cameras on the market.

His second step was to **release the reins**. As this was his third company and the first to reach the highest levels of success, he had kept a tight grip on every area of the organization. He knew he needed to release the reins to succeed, so he restructured the company and his leadership style. Instead of running meetings like pep rallies, ignoring the facts and only focusing on the hype, he was completely transparent with his employees and empowered his leadership team to make decisions on their own that drove longevity instead of instant wins.

As we learned about in mindset shift #3, Nick knew that GoPro needed to **pivot like a pro**. If they wanted to be successful, they couldn't be all things to all people. He had gotten carried away overspending and launching products and service lines that veered too far from GoPro's wearable camera roots. Luckily, he was able to move with agility and pivot like a pro. Instead of continuing to spend like crazy and launch a multitude of mediocre products, he reduced the number of products and ensured they were all the highest quality possible while being maniacally aligned with GoPro's founding mission.

Nick's next step, and mindset shift #4, was to **slow down to speed up**. Now in his midforties, he knows that passion and burning the candle at both ends will get you started but won't carry you, your business, or career through the long term. It took him having night sweats and spiraling into a deep depression to make some serious lifestyle changes. He now blocks out time in his calendar to work out every day, meditate, spend time with his wife, and surf, a lot. He knows he'll never be able to maintain GoPro's success in the long run unless he slows down to speed up and makes taking care of himself a priority.

The final mindset shift and Nick's last step was to **take a victory lap**. Like many successful high achievers, the second he and his team achieved something, he was immediately focused on what was next and how they were going to do it bigger and better next time. He failed to celebrate the wins, which meant that his team often felt like all their hard work was for nothing. Now, instead of hoping for a home run every year, Nick aims for consistent singles and doubles and thoroughly celebrates each milestone and win with the team.

Thanks to the five mindset shifts, Nick has rebuilt his wealth and GoPro. More importantly, Nick is now happier and more aligned in his physical and mental health, his goals, and priorities than ever before. After hitting rock bottom, Nick was able to pull himself out of the vice grip of the Type A Trap, and you can too.

On the one hand, being a Type A personality has given me an incredible life and opportunities I could have only dreamed of, but the Type A Trap has also taken a lot from me. Things I can never replace.

I lost twenty-five embryos during my four failed rounds of IVF due to the stress I was under. That's twenty-five babies that I don't get to meet and love and watch grow up. Twenty-five babies I don't get to hold or cherish. I'll likely never be able to have biological kids of my own. That's a really hard pill to swallow and something I still struggle with every single day.

It took me losing that, nearly losing my job, thousands of dollars in medical bills, a sea of tears, and more to realize that I had to make my physical and mental health a priority. I couldn't just work myself into the ground achieving and achieving but be so broken and depleted that I couldn't enjoy the success or create the thing I wanted most in life—a child of my own.

As my therapist pointedly asked me one day, "Erin, do you want to have a baby or achieve one more thing at work?"

I said, "A baby."

"Then start acting like it," she said.

That stung but made it so clear. Everything I was doing in my life was counter to what I needed to do to get pregnant. But because this Type A behavior was so engrained in my being, I didn't see it. And didn't know how to be any other way.

I don't want you to have to go through some version of what I went through before you realize that you must make yourself a priority. It can't just be about success or putting everyone else first. (I see you, moms.)

So, my question to you is, what are you waiting for? What giant, important life event do you need to miss out on, or person do you need to lose or have walk out of your life before you put yourself first? What's it going to take for you to realize that there's no such thing as doing it all?

If you don't take care of yourself first, you'll never be able to take care of your family, your friends, or your team at work. You'll never be able to reach and sustain peak performance or be an incredible leader without recentering the focus on yourself. Will it take a heart attack, a miscarriage, hitting rock bottom and nearly losing your business like Nick, a divorce, or getting fired before you make yourself a priority?

What if you started to put yourself first today? What would that look like? How would that feel? Start by asking yourself a few questions from our first mindset shift to decode your flow and get laser focused on where you spend your time:

What are you excited about?

What are you curious about?

When do you feel happiest and the most alive?

What thing on your calendar do you look forward to most?

Make a list. Those are the paths to follow and do more of. It's going to look different for everyone, but even making one small adjustment each week of how you spend your time will make a huge difference in your physical and mental health.

So this is my challenge for you today: take five minutes after you finish this book to jot down the answer to these questions while it's all still fresh in your head. Even just getting the answers down on paper and seeing them in writing will make you feel more aligned with your priorities.

Science proves that when we write things down, we're more likely to make them happen. Better yet, post them on social media and tag me (@erinmstafford). Let me cheer you on and hold you accountable. Or share them with a friend and hold each other accountable to making one small adjustment next week. Then one more the week after. If you keep it up, over time, your calendar will better reflect your priorities.

I hope you can start to see how a few small, simple mindset shifts can lead to dramatic, positive changes in your life. When you take care of yourself, you also take care of everyone around you and inspire them to take care of themselves. There is no greater gift in life than our own health. If we don't have that, then nothing else matters.

It's time to take a look in the mirror and realize that the steps we've been taking until now haven't been serving us. It's time to recognize the negative habits that you have and understand that right now, today, you have the steps, a playbook, the know-how, and the ability to create any life that you want. It's possible and you can get started right now.

So, I ask you this: Will you fall victim to the Type A Trap, or will you make adjustments so you can live your life to the fullest and be the absolute best version of yourself?

The time for action is now.

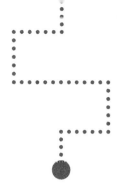

ENDNOTES

An Introduction to Burnout and the Type A Personality

1   Eric Patterson, "Stress Facts and Statistics," *The Recovery Village*, September 5, 2022, https://www.crossrivertherapy.com/stress-statistics-and-facts#:~:text=Around%2033%25%20of%20people%20report,stress%20or%20anxiety%20at%20work.

2   Ayisha Sharma, "What Is a Type A Personality," WebMD, November 9, 2021, https://www.webmd.com/balance/what-is-a-type-a-personality#:~:text=The%20phrase%20%22Type%20A%22%20refers,Motivation%20to%20achieve%20results.

3   Saul McLeod, PhD, "What It Means to Have Type A Personality Traits," accessed January 2023, *Simply Psychology*, https://www.simplypsychology.org/personality-a.html.

4   Ibid.

5   "Depression: What Is Burnout?" National Library of Medicine, June 18, 2020, https://www.ncbi.nlm.nih.gov/books/NBK279286/#:~:text=The%20term%20%E2%80%9Cburnout%E2%80%9D%20was%20coined,ideals%20in%20%E2%80%9Chelping%E2%80%9D%20professions.

6   "Burn-out an 'occupational phenomenon': International Classification of Diseases," World Health Organization, May 28, 2019, https://www.who.int/news/item/28-05-2019-burn-out-an-occupational-phenomenon-international-classification-of-diseases.

7   "Depression: What Is Burnout?" National Library of Medicine, June 18, 2020.

8   Ibid.

9   "Number of quits at all-time high in November 2021," US Bureau of Labor Statistics, January 6, 2022, https://www.bls.gov/opub/ted/2022/number-of-quits-at-all-time-high-in-november-2021.htm#:~:text=Total%20 separations%20increased%20in%20accommodation,first%20produced%20 in%20December%202000.

10   Stefan Ellerbeck, "The Great Resignation Continues. Why Are US Workers Continuing to Quit Their Jobs?" World Economic Forum, January 25, 2023, https://www.weforum.org/agenda/2023/01/us-workers-jobs-quit/.

11   Jack Kelly, "Indeed Study Shows That Worker Burnout Is at Frighteningly High Levels: Here Is What You Need to Do Now," *Forbes*, April 5, 2021, https:// www.forbes.com/sites/jackkelly/2021/04/05/indeed-study-shows-that-worker-burnout-is-at-frighteningly-high-levels-here-is-what-you-need-to-do-now/?sh=58d940db23bb.

12   "8 Employee Engagement Statistics You Need to Know in 2022," *HR Cloud*, June 9, 2022, https://www.hrcloud.com/ blog/8-employee-engagement-statistics-you-need-to-know-in-2021.

Burnout Assessment

1   Dr. Dina Glouberman, *The Joy of Burnout: How the End of the World Can Be a New Beginning* (Makawao: Inner Ocean Publishing, 2003).

Mindset Shift 1: Decode Your Flow

1   Ryan Holmes, "Why This CEO Appointed an Employee to Change Dumb Company Rules," *Fast Company*, March 14, 2017, https://www.fastcompany.com/3068931/ why-this-ceo-appointed-an-employee-to-change-dumb-company-rules.

2   Mark Wilson, "A Eulogy for Every Product Google Has Ruthlessly Killed (145 and Counting)," *Fast Company*, March 22, 2019, https://www.fastcompany. com/90322103/a-eulogy-for-every-product-google-has-ruthlessly-killed-145-and-counting.

3   Mike Isaac, "Meet Facebook's Graveyard of Dead Products," *Vox*, February 25, 2014, https://www.vox.com/2014/2/25/11623922/ meet-facebooks-graveyard-of-dead-products.

4   Jessica Greene-Zapier, "Why It's Better to Be Efficient Rather Than Pro-
    ductive," *Fast Company*, October 29, 2019, https://www.fastcompany.
    com/90423411/why-its-better-to-be-efficient-rather-than-productive.
5   Ibid.
6   Jeff Berger, "Why Every Professional Should Recruit a Personal Board of Advisors,"
    Fast Company, February 17, 2020, https://www.fastcompany.com/90464678/
    why-every-professional-should-recruit-a-personal-board-of-advisors.
7   From Dr. Marsha Chinichian:

    1. Gallup's StrengthsFinder Assessment: In a study of more than two million
       individuals, Gallup found that individuals who used their strengths every
       day were six times more likely to be engaged in their jobs and three
       times more likely to report having an excellent quality of life compared
       to those who did not focus on their strengths.
    2. The Broaden -and -Build Theory: Developed by Barbara Fredrickson,
       this theory suggests that positive emotions broaden an individual's
       momentary thought-action repertoire, which in turn helps build personal
       resources, including resilience, creativity, and problem-solving skills.
       When individuals focus on their strengths, they experience positive
       emotions and can, therefore, build on those personal resources.
    3. The Work of Martin Seligman: Seligman, the father of positive psychology,
       has conducted numerous studies that suggest focusing on one's strengths
       can increase well-being and reduce depression. In one study, he found
       that participants who focused on their strengths and used them in new
       ways had a significant reduction in symptoms of depression.
    4. The Peak-End Rule: This theory suggests that people remember experi-
       ences based on the peak moments and how the experience ended. When
       people focus on their strengths and use them to achieve peak moments,
       they are more likely to remember those experiences positively, leading
       to increased satisfaction and fulfillment.
8   Marcel Schwantes, "Warren Buffett Says 3 Life Choices Separate the Doers
    from the Imposters," *Inc.*, January 20, 2022, https://www.inc.com/marcel-
    schwantes/warren-buffett-says-3-life-choices-separate-doers-from-
    imposters.html.
9   Gary Keller and Jay Papasan, *The ONE Thing: The Surprisingly Simple Truth
    Behind Extraordinary Results* (Austin: Bard Press, 2013).

Mindset Shift 2: Release the Reins

1   Miles Kohrman, "SoulCycle Founders on Learning to Delegate and Becoming Leaders," *Fast Company*, January 15, 2014, https://www.fastcompany.com/3023549/soul-cycle-founders-on-learning-to-delegate-and-becoming-leaders.

2   Kimberly Weisul, "S'well's Founder Knew She Needed to Replace Herself. Here's How She Found the Perfect Person for the Job," *Inc.*, February 26, 2020, https://www.inc.com/kimberly-weisul/sarah-kauss-swell-outside-ceo.html.

3   Ibid.

4   Ibid.

5   Fun fact: I used to work at Stitch Fix back in the day as a stylist. Their systems have definitely evolved since then, but I would choose clothing and accessories for women virtually. It was a great remote styling gig when I was just getting started as a stylist.

6   Elizabeth Segran, "Stitch Fix Sells $1.7 billion of Clothes Each Year. Now, Its Visionary CEO is Passing the Baton," *Fast Company*, April 23, 2021, "https://www.fastcompany.com/90628362/stitch-fix-sells-1-7-billion-of-clothes-each-year-now-its-visionary-ceo-is-passing-the-baton.

7   Stephanie Vozza, "Why This CEO Trained His Employees to Do His Job," *Fast Company*, September 20, 2017, https://www.fastcompany.com/40468078/why-this-ceo-trained-his-employees-to-do-his-job.

8   Alisa Cohn, "Delegating is Great, Except When It's Not," *Inc.*, February 4, 2022, https://www.inc.com/alisa-cohn/delegating-is-great-except-when-its-not.html.

9   Ryan Bradley, "New Belgium Brewery's Employees Think like Owners. Because They Are," *Fast Company*, October 18, 2019, https://www.fastcompany.com/90411668/new-belgium-brewerys-employees-think-like-owners-because-they-are.

10 Ibid.

11 Aaron Hurst, "How Heineken Mexico's CEO Uses Purpose to Unleash the Power of His Organization," *Fast Company*, February 16, 2017, https://www.fastcompany.com/3068060/how-heineken-mexicos-ceo-uses-purpose-to-unleash-the-power-of-his-organiz.

12 Ibid.

13 Ibid.

14 Sarah Ribeiro, "How to Manage Growing Pains during Rapid Team Growth," *Trello*, May 21, 2021, https://blog.trello.com/manage-growing-pains-during-team-growth.

15 Ibid.

16   Marcel Schwantes, "Warren Buffett Says There Is 1 Key Choice in Life That Separates the Doers from the Dreamers," *Inc.*, June 22, 2022, https://www.inc.com/marcel-schwantes/warren-buffett-says-there-is-1-key-choice-in-life-that-separates-doers-from-dreamers.html.

17   Donna Sherriff, "Lean Leadership: How to Loosen the Reins without Losing Your Edge," Bossbabe, accessed March 2022, https://bossbabe.com/author/donna-s/.

18   Ibid.

19   "CliftonStrengths," *Gallup*, accessed April 2023, https://www.gallup.com/cliftonstrengths/en/254033/strengthsfinder.aspx.

20   Elif Suner, "Why Leaders Should Focus on Strengths, Not Weaknesses," *Forbes*, February 6, 2020, https://www.forbes.com/sites/forbescoachescouncil/2020/02/06/why-leaders-should-focus-on-strengths-not-weaknesses/?sh=43d1df553d1a.

21   Ibid.

22   Ibid.

Mindset Shift 3: Pivot Like a Pro

1   "7 Surprising Uses of an ATM," PNC Insights, July 13, 2023, https://www.pnc.com/insights/personal-finance/spend/8-surprising-uses-of-an-atm.html.

2   Blake Ellis, "New ATMs Dispense $1 and $5 Bills," CNN Money, January 17, 2013, https://money.cnn.com/2013/01/17/pf/atm-bills/index.html.

3   Darren Tristano, "Blue Apron, Taking a Cue from Restaurants, Shifts Focus toward On-Demand Consumers," *Forbes*, August 20, 2018, https://www.forbes.com/sites/darrentristano/2018/08/20/blue-apron-shifts-strategy-focus-toward-on-demand-consumers-to-build-meal-kit-revenue/?sh=3ece3b7e473a.

4   Dave Roos, "12 Companies That Completely Reinvented Themselves," HowStuffWorks, February 18, 2022, https://money.howstuffworks.com/10-companies-reinvented-themselves.htm#pt5.

5   Ibid.

6   Bill Whitaker, "The Great Resignation: Why More Americans Are Quitting Their Jobs than Ever Before," *CBS News*, January 9, 2022, https://www.cbsnews.com/news/great-resignation-60-minutes-2022-01-10/.

7   Melissa Angell, "The Real Reasons Workers Are Leaving in Droves? (Burnout Is on the List, but Not at the Top)," *Inc.*, January 25, 2022, https://www.inc.com/melissa-angell/great-resignation-burnout-workers-upskilling-career-development.html.

8   Ibid.

9   Jack Kelly, "What to Do When You Feel Stuck, but Don't Want to Quit Your Job," *Forbes*, February 13, 2022, https://www.forbes.com/sites/jackkelly/2022/02/13/what-to-do-when-you-feel-stuck-but-dont-want-to-quit-your-job/?sh=e5e99c026b89.

Mindset Shift 4: Slow Down to Speed Up

1   Larry Alton, "Are You on the Verge of Burning Out? 7 Warning Signs to Look For (and How to Cope)," *Inc.*, February 21, 2022, https://www.inc.com/larry-alton/are-you-on-verge-of-burning-out-7-warning-signs-to-lookfor-and-how-to-cope.html.

2   Anna Baluch, "Average PTO in the US & Other PTO Statistics (2023)," *Forbes Advisor*, March 30, 2023, https://www.forbes.com/advisor/business/pto-statistics/#:~:text=Over%20765%20million%20vacation%20days%20have%20gone%20unused%20by%20Americans&text=This%20may%20be%20because%20they,too%20much%20to%20get%20done.

3   Robert Glazer, "Why This CEO Pays Employees up to $750 to Unplug on Vacation," *Fast Company*, April 16, 2019, https://www.fastcompany.com/90335109/why-this-ceo-pays-employees-up-to-750-to-unplug-on-vacation.

4   Lydia Dishman, "The Company That Sends Employees on Free International Vacations," *Fast Company*, April 28, 2015, https://www.fastcompany.com/3045491/the-company-that-sends-employees-on-free-international-vacations.

5   Melissa Angell, "Prince Harry and Serena Williams on Dealing with Burnout: Look Inside for the Guidance," *Inc.*, February 7, 2022, https://www.inc.com/melissa-angell/serena-williams-prince-harry-discuss-burnout-betterup.html#:~:text=Their%20conversation%20boiled%20down%20to,%2D%2D%20surely%20feel%20this%20too.

6   Stephanie Mehta, "U.S. Starbucks Employees Can Now Get up to 20 Free Therapy Sessions," *Fast Company*, March 16, 2020, https://www.fastcompany.com/90476917/starbucks-employees-in-the-u-s-can-get-up-to-20-therapy-sessions.

7   Amy Keller Laird, "Why Your Self-Care Methods Aren't Working—and How to Fix That," *Self*, July 20, 2018, https://www.self.com/story/why-your-self-care-methods-arent-working.

Mindset Shift 5: Take a Victory Lap

1   Chris Melore, "It's the Little Things: Average Person Enjoys 4 'Small Wins' Each Day," Study Finds, December 24, 2021, https://studyfinds.org/celebrating-small-wins/.

2   Ibid.

3   Ibid.

4   Teresa M. Amabile and Steven J. Kramer, "The Power of Small Wins," *Harvard Business Review*, May 2011, https://hbr.org/2011/05/the-power-of-small-wins.

5   Ibid.

6   Lindsay Ellis, "Harvard Wants M.B.A.s to Learn How to Be Happy at Work," *Wall Street Journal*, February 14, 2022, https://www.wsj.com/articles/harvard-wants-m-b-a-s-to-learn-how-to-be-happy-at-work-11644836400.

7   Ibid.

8   Ibid.

9   Tris Thorp, "Is Self-Doubt Stopping You from Achieving Your Goals," *Chopra*, September 30, 2019, https://chopra.com/articles/is-self-doubt-stopping-you-from-achieving-your-goals.

10 Ibid.

11 Ibid.

12 Melody Wilding, "How to Brag about Yourself at Work, According to Author and PR Expert Meredith Fineman," *Forbes*, September 15, 2020, https://www.forbes.com/sites/melodywilding/2020/09/15/how-to-brag-about-yourself-at-work-according-to-author-and-pr-expert-meredith-fineman/?sh=2cc78f2f6cc3.

13 Ibid.

14 Ibid.

How the Type A Trap Tests Us

1   Now don't get me wrong. UCLA is an amazing school, and I actually ended up going to summer school there one summer. I love the school. I'm just glad that my path led me to AUP instead.

2   Team Tony, "What Is an Abundance Mindset?" Tony Robbins.com, accessed January 2023, https://www.tonyrobbins.com/mind-meaning/adopt-abundance-mindset/.

3   Ibid.

Type A Trust

1   Mallory Stratton, "6 Incredibly Successful Celebrities Who've Publicly Grappled with Burnout," *Insider*, October 14, 2019, https://www.businessinsider.com/celebrities-who-experienced-burnout-how-they-dealt-with-it-2019-7#6-lilly-singh-6.

2   Ashley Westerman, "New Zealand Prime Minister Jacinda Ardern Plans to Leave Office," *NPR*, January 19, 2023, https://www.npr.org/2023/01/18/1149903191/jacinda-ardern-resignation-new-zealand-prime-minister.

3   Tanya Menon and Leigh Thompson, "Envy at Work," *Harvard Business Review*, April 2010, https://hbr.org/2010/04/envy-at-work.

4   Utkarsh Amitabh, "How to Make Envy Work for You," *Harvard Business Review*, June 8, 2021, https://hbr.org/2021/06/how-to-make-envy-work-for-you.

5   Dr. Kristen Jennings Black, Dr. Christopher J. L. Cunningham, and Dr. Darria Long, "The Burnout Study in Women," Trueve Lab, accessed April 2023, https://trueve.com/wp-content/uploads/2022/10/BurnoutStudy-KeyFindings-1022-v4.pdf?utm_medium=email&utm_source=rasa_io&utm_campaign=newsletter.

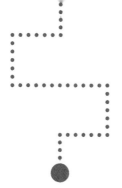

ADDITIONAL RESOURCES

As Type As, and really anyone confronting burnout culture, an insatiable appetite for knowledge empowers us and gives us direction in our shakiest moments. In this section, I share additional resources that I hope will help support you on your journey.

First, make sure you're following me on social media @erinmstafford. I share tools every day to prevent and overcome burnout and ways to stay at peak performance. I also have a lot of fun on there and will be sure to give you a dose of good energy and make you smile.

If you enjoyed *The Type A Trap*, please take a minute to leave a review on Amazon.com. It helps other people just like you find this book and transform their lives.

I mention both of these resources in the text of this book, but here are quick links to them to refer to in future or to share with your friends and colleagues.

- Burnout Toolkit: www.erinstafford.com/toolkit
- Burnout Quiz: www.erinstafford.com/burnoutquiz

There is no shortage of amazing resources on burnout from incredible thought leaders. Here are a few of my favorites:

- *The Joy of Burnout* by Dr. Dina Glouberman
- *Burnout: The Secret to Unlocking the Stress Cycle* by Emily Nagoski and Amelia Nagoski
- *Wonderhell* by Laura Gassner Otting
- *How to Beat Burnout with Gratitude* by M. DE. Carvalho
- *Beating Burnout, Finding Balance* by Melo Calarco
- *Battling Healthcare Burnout* by Thom Mayer, MD
- *The Weary Leader's Guide to Burnout* by Sean Nemecek
- *Burnout Recovery* by Amber Pierce
- *The Burnout Epidemic* by Jennifer Moss
- *Get Out of Your Own Way* by Dave Hollis
- *How Are You Really?* by Jenna Kutcher
- *Healing Burnout* course by Hilary Rushford

I am available to speak at your organization, association, or event. To learn more about working with me, visit erinstafford.com or email hello@erinstafford.com.

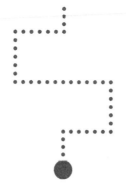

ACKNOWLEDGMENTS

No acknowledgement could start without profusely thanking my parents. I would be nothing without them. Their unconditional love, unwavering support, and constant encouragement have shaped who I am and given me too many blessings to count. I am forever grateful.

To my friends and colleagues at ImpactEleven, you have quickly become some of the best friends I could ask for. The inspiration, support, and community we share leave me pinching myself every day that I get to do this work with you all. Thank you for showing me the way and that it's possible.

To the incredible speakers' bureaus and agents I work with, thank you for believing in me and giving me a platform to share this message so that I can help others escape the Type A Trap.

To the Type A experts who are featured in this book: April Hansen, Ben Nemtin, Bobbie Singh-Allen, Chris Lindsay, Chris Runkle, Danielle Noble, Joe Decker, Keith Karwelies, Lisi Harrison, Martha O'Brasky, Nick Rimedio, Dr. Darria Long, Dr. Madelyn Blair, and Dr. Marsha Chinichian, and the thousands of others I've surveyed and interviewed, thank you for your generosity of time, your insight, perspective, and input. I'm forever thankful.

To Naren and the Amplify team, thank you for believing in me and this message.

To my editor and writing coach, Rebecca Andersen, there are not enough thank yous on the planet to tell you how much I appreciate you. Your help, suggestions, ability to organize my chaotic thoughts, editing, and encouragement are next level. This book would not have been written without you.

To my incredible team and colleagues, thank you for the memories, challenges, laughter, and one hell of a ride. What we accomplished during the pandemic is amazing, and I'm so proud to have done it with you.

To all of the incredible leaders and high achievers I've worked with and known over the years who have shaped my thoughts on burnout and peak performance, thank you for pushing me and inspiring me every day.

To my dog, Baxter, thank you for being the best writing companion and constant cheerleader. Your energy and enthusiasm know no bounds and have forced me to get up and get moving on days I don't feel like it. Thank you for always lifting my mood.

To some of my dearest friends who have helped pull me through the hard times and have been my biggest supporters: Brielle; Jalane; Lauren; Joy; Nick; Brandon; Amanda; Lucy; Elise; Toni; Mim; my Sacramento girls; my brother, Kevin; and of course, my husband, Andrew. Thank you all for believing in me so much.

And to you, the reader, thank you for reading these words and investing in yourself. You bought this book because you thought there had to be a better way to live. I know it's possible, and I hope that, now, you know it too.

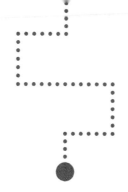

ABOUT THE AUTHOR

Erin Stafford is a marketing guru, burnout survivor, hyper-growth business leader, and social psychologist. While working with the world's highest achievers throughout her twenty-plus-year international career, being a Type A poster child herself, and interviewing Olympians, start-up founders, Fortune 500 CEOs, leading researchers, and celebrity coaches, Erin has seen firsthand how Type A personalities and constant overachievement are coveted in the world of business, but can also lead to debilitating burnout.

After six years heading up marketing for the country's largest healthcare staffing company where she led dozens of marketing professionals and helped the organization grow 900 percent in two years, Erin has made it her mission to help leaders everywhere identify and break free from the Type A Trap so they can stay at peak performance for the long haul.

Erin spends her workweek crisscrossing the globe, inspiring audiences as a keynote speaker. It is her greatest joy and passion to empower individuals and organizations. Her keynotes give audiences the tools and permission to put themselves first, to prevent and overcome burnout, stay at peak performance, and get fired up again, not only about their work, but also about their lives.

If you would like to have Erin speak at your organization or event, visit her website erinstafford.com or email her team at hello@erinstafford.com. Be sure to follow her on Instagram @erinmstafford for a regular dose of good energy, endless tools, and inspiration.

Erin lives in San Diego with her husband and boxer puppy, Baxter.